WALKING THE
THIN BLACK LINE

WALKING THE THIN BLACK LINE

CONFRONTING RACISM IN THE COLUMBUS DIVISION OF POLICE

MELISSA MᶜFADDEN

FIRST EDITION
International Standard Book Number: 979-8-67063-738-1
Library of Congress Control Number: 2020914504

Cover design and book layout by Ben Rossi Designs

To my mother, Arlene Weems, a mighty woman of God, who raised me to have a strong constitution and a keen sense of justice.

October 24, 1946 - April 3, 2020

TABLE OF CONTENTS

ACKNOWLEDGMENTS

To my husband, Charles McFadden, for his love, support, and selflessness. I would not be where I am today without him. To my wonderful son, Isaiah, who has grown up to be a strong, well-rounded man who I am so proud of. To my sisters, Tina Weems, Kimberly Hale, and Pamela Weems, for always having my back no matter where I am in life. I am proud to be their sister. I want to thank my father, Kenneth Weems, my sister, Kenyunda Weems, and the entire Weems family for believing in me and always being there when I needed them. To the Smith and Mays family, for their support and love throughout my life.

I would like to acknowledge the men and women in law enforcement who are just and upright in all their ways and do this job according to God's will. Thanks to the Black officers who came before me and fought this battle, and to all the Columbus Division of Police personnel, past and present, who have given me encouragement, words of wisdom, or just made me smile.

I want to thank Sara Anderson for her wisdom, counsel, and support throughout my career. And thanks to Chris Odom, Joseph Johnson, Chris Smith-Hughes, and Chris Lieb for being wonderful career long friends.

It is a great honor to know Rev. Dr. Jefferey P. Kee, Rev. Dr. Tim Ahrens, Pastor Michael Reeves Sr., Minister Charles Wilson, Cantor Jack Chomsky, Sister Barb Kane, Bishop Donald Washington, Rev. Daniel Clark, Sister Gemma Doll,

Minister Donell Muhammad, Pastor Frederick LaMarr, and the entire Area Religious Coalition (ARC). I want to thank them for standing up against a corrupt, unjust system without asking for anything in return. Different religions, serving one true God, came together to fight against the workers of iniquity. To see the hand of God move through their actions was simply amazing, and I am honored and privileged that God chose me to fight this battle with them.

A special acknowledgment to my contributing editor, Edie Milligan Driskill, for her guidance and assistance in writing this book. She never stopped believing in the power of my story. My amazing editorial team of Diane Stockwell, Katie Caruana, and Benjamin Rossi met impossible deadlines while working with professionalism and grace. Thank you all.

Thank you to Barbara Clark, Kahari Enaharo, Jodi Ann Howell, Joe Motil, Charles Traylor, Larry Wright, and the community for their unwavering support. Finally I want to thank Marshall & Forman LLC, Gittes Law Group, Walton + Brown, LLP, Attorney Bob Fitrakis, and all attorneys who fight for justice.

INTRODUCTION

"No Justice! No Peace!"

You can hear cries for equity ringing out in cities across the world in this summer of 2020 at an unprecedented frequency. If you listen closely, you can hear my cries of resolve and joy among the protesters. It is the most overwhelming feeling to be standing in solidarity with so many young Black activists and their white allies. I never thought I would see a day when I, as a Black officer, could carry a sign for police reform and yell at the top of my lungs what I have always known in my heart—BLACK LIVES MATTER!

After wearing a Kevlar vest for thirty years, I am finally bulletproof while keeping my attorney happily busy filing lawsuits against my employer, the City of Columbus, Ohio. This book is the story of the journey that brought me to this moment when I can speak out without threat of losing my pension.

Many of my Black sisters and brothers in police uniforms in this country have so much to say but find themselves each day balancing speaking their truth against the risk of losing their careers. This is my personal story, but it will resonate through every major city in the United States and perhaps beyond, as they continue to confront the conflicts and pain that permeate their Black communities due to the racism that thrives in their police departments.

As the second Black woman to achieve the rank of lieutenant, the highest rank ever achieved by a Black woman in the history of the Columbus Division of Police, I can finally speak out publicly to defend myself and my Black colleagues against the systemic racism we have endured that has perpetuated the over-policing of African Americans since the era of Reconstruction.

I have worked my entire life for justice. The more I moved up the ranks in the police department, the more I wanted to learn. I have earned my law degree, on top of four other degrees I have accumulated, which affirms my advancement in a system designed to keep me suppressed. As the activists, politicians, journalists, and others debate how to reform policing, the systemic issues Black officers endure are critical to bring to light so that officers and citizens will be able to defeat the racist system that has been virtually untouchable for over 150 years.

Columbus has tragically had more than its share of police violence against Black residents, including killings of unarmed men, killings of children, and other high-profile events that have generated street protests. I have been on the scene at many of those events. But this book is not just about those tragic moments—it's about the culture that creates those actions and allows the officers responsible for the brutality to remain on the job. My story will show how a police department hides its racist policies behind bureaucratic paperwork and staffing strategies. It will explain how they conceal much of that behavior from politicians and even citizens' commissions designed to expose it. It will show

how certain training can create brutal para-militarized officers ready to wage war on Black and poor communities.

With the goal of helping people, I joined the military out of high school to prepare for my lifelong dream of becoming a police officer, but civilian policing is nothing like the military. Police departments buy military-grade equipment to play with but have no respect for its power. We are missing the honor needed as a fighting force to keep us from using these weapons against the same people we are entrusted to serve.

As a Black police officer, I love my community and have dedicated my life to keeping it safe. But my calls for justice, even combined with all the other officers of color in Columbus, are drowned out by the chain of command, the union, and the politicians who are invested in keeping things just the way they are.

Police violence against Black communities has increasingly captured the attention of the public. Activists use a variety of strategies that attract media coverage. However, police officers are normally restricted from sharing their views on the crisis, so our collective perspective is only known from public statements made by our chiefs and media spokespersons. But they do not speak for me.

Activists across the country are aggressively researching policing tactics and police contracts and recommending citizen review boards while lobbying mayors, city councils, and legislatures for change. But because they are understandably suspicious of all police officers, including the Black ones, our perspective is rarely sought out in their research and it is unlikely that they have ever heard our stories.

I am not the first Black officer to take on the City of Columbus and its police department. A class action lawsuit initially filed in 1978 brought the department to its knees under federal supervision. The 1985 judgment corrected many perceived flaws, like the number of Black officers, which increased substantially from under 100 to over 300. However, thirty-five years later, we are back down to only 188 officers out of 1,900 in a city where African Americans make up 28 percent of the population. This is due to the systemic racist hiring practices and targeted attacks on Black officers. We have learned that placing Black officers into a racist system does nothing to change the system but instead does a lot to oppress those officers.

Police reform is one of the most pressing challenges for mayors, city councils, faith leaders, community activists, and voters in general. Everyone is looking for leadership and accurate information to guide their path to solutions. They will not be able to find solutions until they are able to accurately define the problem they are trying to solve. And they won't be able to do that until they get a realistic look inside policing. I have attempted to give you that look through my experience as one very naive young woman from coal country who had no idea how racism could be so virulent—still—today.

Through the lawsuits I've filed, the political process I'm engaging in, technology I'm learning about, community organizing I'm witnessing, and this book I'm writing, I'm seeing a glimmer of hope for Columbus. I invite everyone, especially including the leadership of the Columbus Division of Police, to learn from the experiences in this book to help them live up to their stated commitment to nondiscriminatory law enforcement and personnel practices. I will continue to do what I set out to do—help people while wearing a badge. I hope this book gives you the insight you are missing to join the effort to finally bring all police departments in line with our stated mission—to protect and serve.

AUTHOR'S REFLECTION

Some police officers believe that we are called by God to help the people in our community at their most difficult and dangerous moments. Some wear their uniforms feeling that God ordains police officers to be the authority to enforce His will. Therefore, they believe, if a citizen resists their authority, they are resisting the authority of God and will encounter His wrath.

Several scripture verses are read at police ceremonies and hang on the walls at various officers' workstations that reinforce this belief. This validates their existence as the authority on earth representing God's will.

I believe that God is a just God. He is for justice. He does not discriminate. Throughout my career, I have witnessed injustice and discrimination at the hands of many of these same people who believe they are ordained by God to do this work.

It is not God's will to mistreat people, even those people who mistreat us. As police officers, we have to rise above vengeance and retaliation to be able to do God's work. In our calling, He shows us the way to bring peace to the land, not create hatred and fear.

This memoir is my truth. Police officers across the country each have their own truth, which may or may not be similar to mine. Most officers who have witnessed the mistreatment of citizens and fellow officers are unfortunately not free to share their stories; the officers that use their authority in unrighteous ways suppress the truth.

For he is the minister of God to thee for good. But if thou
do that which is evil, be afraid; for he beareth not the
sword in vain: for he is the minister of God, a revenger
to execute wrath upon him that doeth evil.
Romans 13:4 (King James Version)

1

WHAT WAS
I THINKING?

Early in my career at the Columbus Division of Police, my fellow officers labeled me a troublemaker. My future as a disruptor was launched.

"We have to get out of here," my Black field training officer, Linda, whispered urgently as we drove past a fellow police officer conducting a traffic stop on the near east side of Columbus, a predominantly Black neighborhood. It was late one Thursday night in 1997, and we had slowed down to see if Dave, the white officer on the stop, needed any assistance. We could see the driver sitting in the back seat of the police cruiser, parked a short distance away, while his car was being searched. Suddenly, we realized we needed to leave.

The trunk of the car was open, and we could see Dave rifling through it. But we knew Dave didn't have consent from the driver to search the car. To give consent, a driver needs to be close enough to the car to verbally terminate or limit the scope of the search at any time—this driver certainly couldn't do that while locked in a cruiser parked ten feet away. If any evidence of a crime was discovered, even a bad defense attorney could get the case thrown out.

This is a common practice. It goes like this: An officer pulls over a car for a traffic stop. Even if the stop is legitimate, they still need a valid reason to search the vehicle. If they don't have a reason, they ask the driver for consent. The driver is then told to wait in the cruiser while the officer searches the car, unaware that they have the right to watch the search and stop it at any time.   If the officer finds anything, like narcotics or illegal firearms, then they make an arrest. If they don't find anything, the officer often releases the driver with no ticket or charges filed.

This was the first time I had seen this happen, but it wasn't the first time for my training officer. I had learned a lot from Linda—I both respected and liked her. She cared about her job and had trained me well. She was a good officer in a bad system, with eight years on the job with the Columbus Division of Police. She knew enough to realize that if we had stayed on the scene that night, we could have been implicated in the illegal search if the driver had filed a complaint with the Internal Affairs Bureau (IAB), the officers assigned to police the police. She also knew that complaining about the officer conducting the illegal search or trying to correct the situation would only come back on us. We would catch hell. Maybe not official hell, but the kind that would make it difficult to be an officer. So we left the scene.

At twenty-seven and just out of the police academy, I was so young. I was only three years out of the US Air Force, where I had served as a security police (SP) for four years. In the military, rules had kept me safe. Rules were there to keep everyone safe—and, most importantly, alive. We had all lived by the same code of conduct, knowing that code would come down on us just as hard when we saw a violation and didn't report it as it would if we had done the crime ourselves.

But there I was, driving past a routine traffic stop where another officer was breaking a rule—an essential one, and a constitutional rule that was in place to maintain our civil liberties. Now I was being trained to look the other way: I thought to myself, *Don't make waves. Don't make anyone angry, especially an officer with more experience.* Compared to me, that was just about everyone at that moment. I wasn't even done with my field training.

I was figuring out pretty quickly that I wasn't in the military anymore. My training officer was showing me that they left a lot out of the training manual. I must have been naive, but I had no idea that police officers broke laws and covered up for each other. I didn't know there was a thin blue line that ruled how officers worked with each other, a code that said we had a personal duty to each other, not just a duty to our job. I hadn't learned this in the military, and I certainly hadn't in the police academy. These were the skills I learned by watching the more experienced officers.

Looking back, I now realize the driver subjected to the search that night probably didn't know his legal rights. In the unlikely event that he even knew how to complain or where to lodge a complaint, he most likely guessed (correctly) that if he did file a complaint, things would just get worse for him, and the IAB would find a way to justify the officer's actions. And that would be that.

As illegal searches continued, all the other officers went on pretending not to notice. Toward the end of my second phase of training, which would be my last if everything went well, Linda took a well-deserved vacation day. That night at roll call, I was about to be temporarily assigned to ride with another officer for the shift. I looked across the room at Dave, and images of me starring in a hit reality TV show, *Crooked Cops of Columbus*, flashed before my eyes. Not me, no way! So I spoke up and pointed at Dave. "I don't want to ride with him." The shift supervisor asked me why. "He conducts illegal searches," I answered without thinking.

I must have been out of my mind to say that out loud. But I had never been in an environment where telling the truth would be the wrong thing to do. So there I was, announcing to the entire room of maybe seven officers that I wasn't going to look the other way when I saw an injustice go down. After all, I hadn't planned to become an officer and wear a uniform with pride for my entire life just to have it tarnished by the bad behavior of a few.

This was a milestone moment for me and my efforts to enforce the notion that cops should actually follow the rules. The moment was so memorable, in fact, that a Facebook group of Columbus officers brought up my comment twenty-one years later in 2018—when I was publicly going after the latest incident of mis-policing. A friend who was part of the group sent me the screenshot.

In that single moment back in 1997, not only did I learn that I would be resisting a rampant cover-up culture, but I was also forever tagged as the poster child for going against the status quo, way before Facebook tagging even existed.

Since before anyone can remember, Columbus police have made an art form out of squelching citizen complaints. As an example, when Chief Kimberley Jacobs (2012 - 2019) became chief, she removed the deputy chief in charge of the IAB so they reported directly to her. This gave her more direct access to internal affairs investigations and greater influence over the outcomes of any complaints.

She wanted to make sure her department looked clean, even though it was far from it. She had a long-standing tradition to uphold. In my twenty-four years with the department, there has been exactly one racial profiling complaint sustained (which means upheld), and it was— unbelievably—against a Black officer, in 2001, who was then fired.

But back in 1996, when I entered the academy, I didn't see the racism at first. I know that sounds unusual coming from a Black woman who grew up in West Virginia, but I had experienced no evidence of discrimination during my four years in the US Air Force. Everyone got the same abusive treatment from their basic training instructors and received the required training to be successful airmen. Though it may have been different in other military divisions or locations, everyone in my basic training unit at Lackland

Air Force Base in San Antonio endured the same discipline for bad behavior, and our military culture didn't give us time to look for arbitrary external differences. We were all the same—young recruits, green on the inside with a lot to learn. We all trained hard together, followed the rules, or took our punishment when we didn't.

After graduating high school in 1988, I had chosen to enlist in the military instead of going to college, and I opted for military police assignments over other possible career paths for one reason: at age fourteen, I had decided to be a police officer. Somewhere, I had gotten the notion that the military would prepare me for that goal. But the illegal search I saw on that momentous Thursday night in 1997 would never have happened in my military unit. First off, such an important rule wouldn't have been broken. Second, if it had, other airmen would have immediately reported it. Third, they wouldn't have feared any retaliation for following the rules and expecting their fellow airmen to do the same.

For a hot second, my first attempt at resisting corruption looked like it was working. After speaking up at roll call, I was assigned a temporary partner who wasn't Dave. Later that night, we responded to a call at a home where a woman reported a man trying to break in through her patio door. We rolled up just as Danielle, another Black female officer, arrived. Danielle and I took the front while our partners went around to the back of the house. We positioned ourselves at either side of the front door, as we had been trained to do as a safety precaution. The resident opened the door, and Danielle and I went right in while the officers in the back rushed in through the patio door at the same time. We all cleared the area, determining that the suspect had already left. So the call was resolved with everyone's safety intact.

A few days later, just when I didn't need it, I found myself under review for officer safety issues. This could impact my training schedule and require me to complete an extra third phase, or six more weeks, of field training. I was livid because a third phase would mean they were looking for a way to terminate me. I did not have any incidents where I had put another officer or myself at risk, either during my training with the police department or in my four years in the military. The case in question concerned the back-door intruder—I was accused of standing directly in front of the front door.

I was so confused—until I figured out this was retaliation for speaking out about the illegal searches. I explained to the field training coordinator, in a meeting at his office, what I had said at roll call. I told him that I hadn't received any negative evaluations in both phases of training until after the night I spoke up about the illegal searches. He must have believed me because he did not send me to a third phase of training.

The charge of "officer safety issues" is to a police officer what the accusation of "disorderly conduct" or "obstructing official business" is to a Black man at the wrong place at the wrong time—it's a catch-all offense they use when nothing else fits, or when there isn't really a conduct violation. When supervisors want to mete out an undeserved punishment or harass an officer so they will eventually transfer, quit, or be terminated this charge works very well—it can mean anything they want it to mean.

Most surprising to me was that Danielle was helping with the charge against me. I later learned that her motivation was some sort of payback because she heard an untrue rumor about me dating a guy in the academy. (What was this, middle school?) We later became friends and supportive colleagues once we realized that there were too few Black women in the police division for any of us to hold grudges against one another. Our issues with discrimination were so difficult, it was a gift to have others who immediately understood what we were going through.

Looking back years later, I realize that when Linda heard about how I had spoken up at roll call, she was mortified. She had worked so hard to help me fit into this culture that she didn't totally agree with but also couldn't change. She had done her job and trained me well—but the other officers didn't see it that way after what I said. After that roll call incident, Linda never spoke to me again. She understood how to keep herself safe within the corrupt culture.

I had just learned two valuable lessons: First, I now understood that retaliation was real, and hard to prove. Second, I knew I couldn't let my career be guided by threats of retaliation. Before I was even done with my training, I had already been labeled as a troublemaker. But even that reputation wasn't enough to shake my military training and upbringing, which had taught me to follow rules and do the right thing. I was totally committed to holding onto that moral compass throughout this early challenge to my values.

At the same time, police departments were about to embark on a brand-new era in their post-9/11 history. We would have access to more and more equipment and strategies originally designed for military operations. The term "para-militarization of police forces" is now commonly heard and discussed as one of the main problems with policing in the last decade. Those military tools can't work without the structure and discipline that comes from actual military training. The six months I spent at the police academy was valuable, but the academy can't turn out soldiers or sailors or airmen with the same respect for the power they possess that the military can in the time they spend training each recruit.

One key difference is that in the military we all go to basic training and then go directly into a specialty where we have training that is designed to develop competence in that specialty. A police academy is like basic training in that we all get the same course of instruction, but that is where the similarity ends. From there we all go straight to the Patrol Bureau. Each time we transfer into a different assignment later, we receive our specialized training on the job.

Another key difference is that police academies ultimately turn out officers with little respect for the power of the weapons they are given. More importantly, academy graduates don't have the same respect for their fellow officers or for the community they serve as the military does. As military police in the US Air Force, we were members of the community we served—it was our job to keep everyone safe and mission-ready. We didn't see the folks we came in contact with as "others." They were us. We treated them with the same respect with which we would treat our own families. I didn't see a similar culture of respect for the community being developed in the police department.

During my rookie year, I continued to do my job, learn from my colleagues, and witness behavior that didn't make any sense to me. Toward the end of that year, I was at a training class where white male officers were teaching us how to conduct a felony stop. These techniques would be used, for example, when pulling over a suspect in a bank robbery. The training officers started by explaining that if you had a suspect playing loud music with their baseball cap on backwards, you should use your microphone/ loudspeaker. They went on to demonstrate that if the suspect's pants were sagging, you should just grab the back of their pants to pull them out of the car with, "Get out here, BOY!"

With that phrase, I suddenly realized that racism in the police department was a reality. The words jumped out at me like a zombie in a house of horror. What the hell?! Any adult man would be insulted to be called a "boy," but when someone yells this at a Black man, it evokes centuries of racist history.

Then I thought back through their profile of this fictional suspect: loud music, baseball cap on backwards, pants sagging. They wanted us to see a Black man in our minds. Crap, these guys were racist! I felt so naive for not having recognized it before. But it was clear as glass to me now. Before this training, I thought all actions were about what was legal and illegal, but this example showed me that race was a factor in how police officers were being trained to treat suspects.

I immediately wrote Sergeant Brian Bruce, the defensive tactics leader at the time, and shared my shock and disgust that the trainers explicitly suggested using the word "boy" to speak to a grown man, and explained the racial connotations of that word. He assured me he would correct the problem. He didn't owe me more than that, so I never found out if he did speak to the trainers or how that conversation went. But I felt like I was back in the military: I had witnessed something that would put everyone at risk and that wouldn't be an appropriate behavior for a well-trained police officer. I felt it was my responsibility to report it. So I did.

And so began over twenty years of me being a pain in everyone's backside. I knew I couldn't simply look the other way, especially when Black or women police officers were discriminated against or when citizens were harassed or mistreated. But I also knew the power that was the Columbus Division of Police, a system that had survived a federal class action lawsuit a dozen years earlier, was found guilty of multiple acts of discrimination, and was fast returning to the same den of discrimination it had been before the lawsuit.

I was only one rookie officer, a woman, and an African American at that. I wasn't from Columbus, so I had no community to count on here for support. I knew I had no power at that time to change a system that was so entrenched. It was also clear to me that I wouldn't even survive if I didn't start reinforcing my position. So I hunkered down.

Even though candidates don't need more than a GED to be accepted into the police academy and most of my fellow officers didn't have much college education themselves, I chose education as my path to job security in my career. I had been enrolled in community college while waiting to be accepted into the police academy, so I took classes until I got my associate of arts degree from Columbus State Community College in 2002. In 2004, I received a bachelor of arts degree in criminology and bachelor of social work from Capital University, and I followed that up with a master's degree in criminal justice from Tiffin University. Finally, in 2018, I received my juris doctorate in law from Capital University Law School. I found classes to fit in around my full-time shifts at work. There were many nights when my son and I did our homework together.

These academic degrees gave me tremendous insights into my career, the people I serve, the law itself, and the injustices that are handed out by police departments across the country. But they also gave me credibility that I thought couldn't be challenged. As a Black woman, I had to work harder and smarter than my peers. The challenge didn't faze me—I liked the work, and I wanted to do it well. But when that additional effort was still not enough to gain the respect, assignments, and advancement I saw other officers getting, I needed a résumé that I thought couldn't be challenged. So I went out and got one.

I also needed a good attorney on speed dial. I filed my first discrimination lawsuit against the City of Columbus in 2003. I learned that the Fraternal Order of Police (FOP), our police union, didn't have my back as the person discriminated against. So I focused on the only thing I have trusted my whole life other than God and my mother: rules. We have lots of them, and when the Columbus Division of Police ignores or breaks one, I don't hesitate to point it out and seek legal remedies. My time in law school has made that even easier.

Other officers who suffered discrimination saw what I was doing and sought out my unofficial advice and counsel. I then began experiencing retaliation for my support of these officers. Their stories, which you'll learn about in the following chapters, underscore even more deeply how entrenched the racist culture is. Hearing the stories of how young Black men and women are unfairly treated by an employer that supposedly creates equal opportunities is provoking enough. But these same officers must also witness discriminatory and violent acts waged on the poor communities and communities of color that they serve and supposedly protect. Often they must actively participate in this discrimination themselves, in order to keep advancing their careers.

This is where I tell you that not all Black police officers are perfect. And not all Black police officers agree with me 100 percent. That's just about being different human beings—everyone has different strategies for coping with a corrupt system. But we all work for a corrupt system, and we all experience different pieces of it while serving as police officers.

I quickly became a mentor to other officers experiencing internal challenges within the division. As I moved up the ladder, more and more officers came to me for help. Recently even white men have sought my help when they have gotten into trouble.

As a teenager dreaming of being a police officer, I didn't know that I would be fighting a system of oppression much older than the institution of policing. As a Black woman, I experience both racism and sexism, and it's often hard to tell which is at work. There are certainly women and Black officers who have held positions of leadership, including chief of this police department. But I've seen that even these leaders have no real power against long-established systems that reinforce and even propagate illegal actions against officers and citizens.

Our political leaders, the media, activists, citizen watchdog groups, faith leaders, academics, and everyone else who studies policing can't see what Black and female police officers see. But we aren't allowed to speak our truth— at least, not without retaliation. And even then, it's hard to know how to defend ourselves against that retaliation without coming off as just another angry Black woman.

I admit it: I am angry. Throughout this story, you will connect with some of my anger. And then again, sometimes you won't. But it's not about whether I have a right to be angry or not. It's about making sure others don't have to experience the same anger in the future. Because the crap that happens that I'm angry about hurts everyone.

You have no doubt had an unfair boss at one time or another. You may have watched a customer get mad over poor service where you worked, and you felt helpless to change the rules. You surely must have had at least one coworker who cut corners and made your job harder. This is normal in most workplaces. But in policing, these issues can turn into civil rights violations, resulting in unjust arrests, injuries, or even death.

As Black police officers, we see the injustice waged against communities of color every day. At the same time, some members of those communities view Black officers as traitors. That hurts, but we have to walk that thin black line. On one side of the line, we are responsible for protecting our community from unjust police action. On the other, we are responsible for protecting ourselves from a discriminatory work environment. For over twenty years, I have looked for ways to eliminate racism within the Columbus Division of Police, and I'm certain of one thing: we can't truly stop the war against marginalized communities until we clean up our own house.

It took twenty-two years, but I finally arrived at the moment where I could begin to affect real change. In October of 2018, when I turned forty-eight, I added my four years of military service and one year from Ohio State to my time as a police officer and filed for retirement under the Ohio Police and Fire Pension. I then reinvested my benefits in their deferred retirement option plan, which allowed me to continue to work. Before that date, there were two efforts waged against me to invoke the clause that could have caused me to lose my entire pension. It reads:

> If you have fewer than 25 years of service credit and were discharged from the police or fire department due to dishonesty, cowardice, intemperate habits, or conviction of a felony, no pension benefits can be paid under state law.

However, those attempts were unsuccessful, and I can now speak openly because my financial future is secure. I worry about my community that is still searching for a sense of security. I care about other minority officers who walk the thin black line daily. My real sense of security will only come when every police officer in the country can call out injustice without fear, until we get to that night when there is none left to call out.

2

WHO WOULDN'T
WANT TO BE A COP?

With Cagney and Lacey as my only role models, I headed to
the Air Force for what I thought would be the best training to be
a cop—a profession I thought was all about helping people.

Price Hill, West Virginia, an unincorporated village on the outskirts of Mount Hope (pop. 1400), was an odd place to grow up. It was originally built in the 1890s by a coal company 2400 feet up into the Appalachian Mountains. In eighth grade we moved ten miles down Route 19 to Beckley (pop. 20,000). The next biggest city was the capital, Charleston (pop. 50,000), sixty miles north.

We weren't totally cut off from mainstream America, but I would say we were a little behind. We had a very simple, very poor life grounded in family and religion. I was in the middle of four sisters, and we fought, well, like sisters. They thought I was nuts because I wanted to be a cop and they couldn't imagine why. I thought they were crazy for not wanting to pursue that amazing career. We were raised mostly by our mom, who always wanted the best for us and emphasized the importance of church, education, hard work, and helping people. I thought of police officers as the most powerful helpers in a community. When someone was in distress, they were always the first to arrive to make them safe. If I couldn't be a cop, I told my young self, I'd be a social worker.

When I graduated from Woodrow Wilson High School in 1988, I was just as idealistic as most eighteen-year-olds, and even more invincible than most. I had not given up on my lifelong goal, but the path to becoming a police officer for a little Black girl from West Virginia was not so clear. I always looked for the next opportunity to improve, so the military seemed like a good place to gather the skills necessary to be a good officer.

My mom and my church instilled in me a strong sense of right and wrong. Because of them, I also have a keen sense of justice. I can't stand injustice, even against people I might not personally like, or who may have even harmed me in the past. The military had a similar set of standards, and I got along well in that culture. They made it crystal clear what was wrong, so I was very comfortable following the rules.

One time during my four years in the military I was subjected to an Article 15, the process of investigating a crime or rule infraction in the military justice process. While stationed in Michigan, my superior officer asked me to do a special assignment with the Office of Special

Investigations, the military equivalent of the Internal Affairs Bureau at a police department. They told me they needed me for an undercover operation. I was told to take a flak jacket to a local military surplus store and try to sell it. I knew it was against the rules to sell our military equipment. I understood that the investigators wanted to find out if the store owner would purchase the flak jacket.

During this assignment, I was sharing a locker with Lisa, another Black airman. We stored our gear together. It turned out that Lisa had taken my jacket into the same store to sell for cash. The investigators really wanted to find out if the store owner recognized me so they could rule me out. Knowing what I know now about investigations, this was actually a compliment. I could have been called into the investigation as a suspect directly, instead of being given the benefit of the doubt and asked to help with it.

When I went to the store, the owner didn't recognize me, of course, but because I was under investigation, I wasn't allowed to deploy to Korea—where I had been thrilled to be assigned. I was so mad about it and raised such a big fuss to go overseas that they deployed me to Turkey instead. Lisa was discharged for theft of government property, just like that. The military doesn't have time for nonsense or excuses or even second chances. You learn the rules, you follow the rules, and you respect your fellow officers.

Throughout my tour with the US Air Force, I served as a security specialist. This assignment gave me a wonderful foundation that I still build on today. I had never carried a gun before, but they taught me to fire a variety of weapons.

I advanced to become an armorer, maintaining weapons and outfitting other troops. I also served as an entry control operator, checking credentials for access to secure areas. These assignments helped me advance above the ground level, by mastering specific skills. This type of training helped me to become a dispatcher while in Turkey for twelve months, delegating assignments to my peers.

The overall experience solidified the work ethic instilled in me while growing up. I learned how to apply my talents in a team setting, know my part, and pull my own weight. I learned how hierarchical management structures work and became comfortable with the concept of rank. But I can't stress enough that I saw how learning and following the rules was the key to everything working well and no one getting hurt.

In my first assignment out of basic training, I was stationed at Wurtsmith Air Force Base in Oscoda, Michigan. I was one of only two female airmen in a flight of fifty. We were divided into various posts to include a fire team of four that would respond to fence alarms that went off in the controlled areas on the base. I worked the third shift, which was usually pretty quiet and only had one team working. So three guys and I would wait for alarms. The base housed nuclear uploaded B-52 bombers and mission silos. It was our job to protect them. We would go out for any fence alarms, to check the perimeter to maintain security.

It had only been a little over two years since 1986, when females had first been given this assignment in the US Air Force. There were still pictures of naked women stuck in the procedure training books, and they had a Showtime subscription so they could watch R-rated movies with partial nudity while waiting in the fire team building to be called out.

I was raised as a Christian, and this didn't feel right to me at all. I told my superior officer that I was uncomfortable with the naked women, and he made sure all that material was removed. I was young and didn't understand at the time what a pivotal point this was in the history of women's expanding role in the military. I was in the first wave of women who needed to point out things like this, but my chain of command was ready to respond to my request. As the command changed, the culture changed as commanded.

When I was honorably discharged from the military in December of 1992 I headed to Columbus, Ohio, because my older sister and my mom had moved here from West Virginia for better opportunities. Columbus is the capital of Ohio and had just surpassed Cleveland to become the largest city in the state when I got here. It is home to Ohio State, one of the largest universities in the country, and several national corporate headquarters. It is now the fourteenth largest city in the US with almost one million people, and is by some accounts the only one still growing in the Midwest. We are expected to reach a population of three million by 2050. Ohio shares a border with West Virginia, which has encouraged a lot of migration to Columbus over the years. With our growth we are also seeing a healthy increase in our Black community and our immigrant communities, including many from Latin countries, Asia, and Africa. But like most cities in the northern US, as Black families arrived during the Great Migration, we were segregated through redlining. Those neighborhood distinctions persist today, with the east side of town housing many of the 28 percent of residents who are Black.

Columbus has a large police department with over 1,900 sworn officers and our own police academy. When I got here, I signed up for the test to enter the academy and started working as a security officer at a warehouse in town. On a cold day in 1994, I sat for the test for the first time. I remember nothing about the questions except that I answered enough correctly to land in the ninety-fifth percentile—only five people out of a hundred who took the test did better than me. That felt pretty good. I was used to getting good grades, but this test was the most important one I'd ever taken, the first step in realizing the dream I'd had for most of my life. It was very exciting.

I went into the interview at police headquarters following the exam with confidence. Surely my high score would impress them. They let me know that in my background check they had spoken to a previous supervisor at the warehouse, who also happened to be an ex-boyfriend, who said I was insubordinate at work. Another supervisor at the same company said I was a fine employee, but my ex-boyfriend was more interesting to my interviewers. So we talked about him for a while.

It was beginning to feel like all the hard work and commendations I had received in the military were not going to count for anything. They had received my personnel records that had reviews like:

> A1C Weems is an outstanding example of what an airman should strive to be. Though not in a position of specific leadership responsibility, she leads by example. A1C Weems excels in professional military knowledge and projects a truly professional image. This resulted in her winning the squadron's Airman of the Month for June '90. She received a 97.5 percent on her Quality Control Evaluation for Response Force Member. A1C requires little supervision and performs all tasks in a timely manner with quality results.
> -- 3 Nov '90

But it didn't seem to matter.

Seemingly out of nowhere, I was disqualified because they learned from my background check that I owed $79 to the IRS for my 1992 tax return and had two traffic tickets on my record. Did this really mean I couldn't be trusted to enforce the laws and serve the citizens of Columbus, Ohio?

It did occur to me that I might be experiencing discrimination, especially when I later learned that applicants with cocaine possession on their records had been accepted. I had never been accused of a crime, let alone convicted. But I didn't question the rules of authority—not even this one. Nor did I have any idea that I could complain about a violation of the equal employment opportunity laws. It was disheartening, but I wasn't going to let it stop me.

It would be about a year before I could sit for the test again, so I enrolled in Columbus State Community College and got a new job at The Ohio State University hospital as a security guard. I was waiting for the next opportunity to be accepted into the police academy.

After my second good grade on the test, I was ready to get on with it. The first step was the polygraph test, designed to make sure we weren't lying in our applications. I appreciated that level of investigation, knowing I would be working alongside others who had also been thoroughly screened. But they hit me with a question I hope you've never heard in any interview you've ever had: "Have you ever been involved in any incestual relationships?" The answer is no, not that it's any of your business either. But I froze for an uncharacteristic second, realizing that I was being stereotyped because of my West Virginia heritage. Shock, anger, disbelief, and confusion all took their turns in rapid succession while I tried to stay focused on the rest of the questions. As a trained military police officer, I knew how to do that—I could keep my cool and do my job in the face of an enemy trying to throw me off my game.

The day I showed up for my oral boards, I was terribly nervous after the insulting polygraph question. The officers that interviewed me were a little intimidating, even though it was slightly reassuring to see one Black man and one woman on the panel. I normally felt confident in settings like this, but I was feeling more pressure since they had rejected me the year before. They seemed to go straight to the intimidating questions about drugs and alcohol. When they learned I had never smoked weed and didn't drink, they seemed disappointed, like they were looking to dismiss my application again.

Then they wanted to talk about the two traffic tickets I had gotten in my life. It was beginning to feel a lot like they really were looking for a reason to ignore my performance on the exam or the fact that I was now current on all my taxes. How could I win at this game when they were looking for any reason to get rid of the little Black girl from the hillbilly state?

I left feeling like I was never going to be accepted. They said nothing that made me think they respected me or were interested in me becoming a police officer. So imagine my excitement when I learned that I had been accepted into the academy. Had they just been trying to make me feel inadequate? Or was it a way to sort out those who couldn't take the insults? It didn't occur to me at that time that my growing sense of being discriminated against would continue throughout my entire career. I thought that the people who interviewed me were just ignorant or biased, or testing me to make sure I could stand up for myself. They eventually learned the hard way that I could.

I entered the Columbus Police Academy on May 19, 1996, and graduated in November of that year. Columbus held classes with around fifty recruits two or three times per year then. There were forty-five recruits in my class, seven of us Black. Twenty-seven of us still work for the division, two of us Black. In our little sample, we went from 15 percent to 7 percent Black at a time when the Black population of Columbus increased from less than 18.5 percent to almost 30 percent. Other academy classes haven't kept up with changing demographics either.

Sergeant Ronald Stevens, an African American, was the training officer at the time. His being Black didn't affect me one way or the other. The military culture I had experienced was about as race neutral as anyone would want it to be in order to learn and do a good job. I had received good training from both Black and white military training instructors.

Even though Sergeant Stevens had not been in the military, he and other academy training officers tried to train people using military-style tactics including yelling, push-ups, and all the standard stuff you see on TV shows. But that's about where it stopped.

Being ex-military, I expected certain things. In the military we had a buddy system and it was our job to make sure everybody succeeded. We always made sure everyone was okay, and we certainly didn't do anything to hurt or insult each other.

I surely didn't expect the totally opposite approach I found in the police training academy. Sergeant Stevens would pick on people for random reasons, and sometimes, it seemed, only because he just didn't like them. He would target certain people to mistreat. Then some of the class members would follow his lead and add their own bullying. I felt that because they knew I had been in the real military, they didn't pick on me. But watching others endure this unjust treatment was just as uncomfortable.

There was a particular week in the training academy called hell week, when the recruits were forced to wrestle and box with each other. Unlike professional matches with different weight classes, the trainers purposefully assigned us to mismatched bouts, like a man fighting a woman half his size. When I went through the academy, people from all over the division would come and watch the boxing matches, making it a rite of passage. Because the officers who came to watch had been through it, they thought everyone should go through it. But it had become a hazing, with recruits getting hurt. Broken noses and cracked ribs were not unusual. The injured recruits would then need more time to finish their training, but it was just a part of the process.

As time went on, the trainers decided to close off the fighting to outsiders. Maybe society was changing and it just wasn't cool anymore to let others see how ridiculous they were behaving. Now, instead, each recruit had to be maced and tased. The theory was that when a recruit gets maced she gains confidence in its effectiveness, so she will be more likely to trust it with an aggressive suspect and not choose a higher level of force. Officially, the tasing is now voluntary, but the recruits experience so much peer pressure that it feels mandatory. As a substitute for the live boxing events, the training officers record the recruits being tased and then pass around the videos. The recruits have to experience officers publicly laughing and ridiculing them. The hazing has gone high-tech.

I have never understood why the training academy has a swimming pool, other than as another tool to haze the recruits. Even recruits who can't swim have to get in the water. There is no swimming instruction in the curriculum—I couldn't swim when I was accepted to the academy, and still can't. Water rescues are not part of the normal job description, like they might be for firefighters and paramedics.

Several years later, when I worked at the training academy, I had an office facing the courtyard. The recruits were out there and I saw them taking something and putting it to their mouths, passing it back and leap over the next recruit, through the whole line of recruits. I asked a training officer what was going on. Sergeant Stevens had placed a Honey Bun in the locker room but claimed that he found it there. Since the recruits were not supposed to be eating junk food, to make a point he made them eat the Honey Bun, all putting it in their mouths while playing leap frog. It seemed totally ridiculous and surely could be considered hazing.

In the military the approach was the complete opposite. We were there to support each other, and everyone was treated the same. They tore you down with the goal to build you back up. In the police academy, the only goal was to tear us down to watch us fail. There was no reason for this—the academy is not where recruits should be weeded out. We had already gone through extensive background checks, tests, medical and physical exams, interviews and polygraphs. We were ready to be good police officers, and the only goal of the academy should be to make sure that happens.

It's no wonder that a lot of citizen complaints include rudeness and mistreatment, since we were taught this behavior in the academy. The trainers rationalize the physical abuse with the notion that we need to feel what it's like to be hit in the face before we get hit on the street. But on the street, if we get hit, it's never a boxing match because we have other tools to end the fight quickly (like mace and tasers). Letting some dude twice my size break my ribs in the academy doesn't mean that I am better prepared to survive on the street.

The military's goal is to build up the character and the skills of the recruits so we will excel in our duties. But the instructors at the police academy are not trained in military concepts. They use whatever random strategies that their instructors used, with a few tips from *Full Metal Jacket* for effect. There is no psychology or pedagogy behind it. In the military, they study the outcomes of their training policies to make sure they are effective, and do certain things for certain reasons. The academy is not versed in how to build an officer using military tactics.

One system the academy has borrowed from the military is called "gig slips." These are blank pieces of paper with our name on them that we are required to carry at all times. If we make a mistake or break a rule, a supervisor will ask for a slip and fill it in with our infraction. We cannot graduate from the academy if we lose all of our slips.

In my class at the academy there was a Black recruit named Daniel. Sergeant Stevens didn't like him for some reason and gave him silly assignments as punishments, like washing cars. The rules were applied inequitably to him. He lost all his gig slips, so in solidarity the entire class each donated one of our slips to him. We gave them to another training officer to give to Sergeant Stevens, who proclaimed that he didn't care at all about our slips, threw them up in the air, and walked out of the room. Our action was intended to show our support for our classmate, whom we all felt was being mistreated.

Some officers who graduated from the police academy have true disdain for their instructors, because they feel some of the tactics used were personal attacks on them. I know several officers who still feel this way years later. This is not how any officer should feel at the end of their training. In the military we knew that the training instructor was doing her job, and we respected her for that. We felt stronger for it in the end, not weaker.

3

1985 LAWSUIT
CHANGES NOTHING

Way before I entered the academy, a class action lawsuit had proven rampant
discrimination throughout the Columbus Division of Police and mandated new
policies to fix it. They just got better at hiding it.

I first learned of the lawsuit after I graduated from the
academy. It certainly hadn't made the news in Beckley,
West Virginia, and they did not cover it in the curriculum
at the police academy. I had no idea how much struggle had
come before paving the way for me to seek this career until
after the academy, when this history was slowly revealed.
That's when I joined Police Officers for Equal Rights (POER),
an organization made up of African American officers from
Columbus who had filed a lawsuit.

The case, Police Officers for Equal Rights versus the City of
Columbus, was filed in 1978, around the time I was learning
my multiplication tables and fighting with my sisters over

who had to do the dishes. The case developed over the next six years, just as I was developing my admiration for police officers and planning to become one. I had no inkling of the additional respect I would feel as I learned of the abuse Black officers in Columbus had endured on the job—I couldn't have imagined what they risked to fight for their rights and citizens' rights. I also had no idea how much of that battle would be left for me to wage.

A lot of people think of the 1960s as when the most important civil rights battles were fought in our country. But a lot of the judicial tests of the Civil Rights Act of 1964 were not hammered out until the 1970s. Columbus was one of the first school districts to receive a federal court order to desegregate. The busing order was handed down by Federal Judge Robert Duncan in March of 1977, and the first students boarded the crosstown buses in September of 1979. The white students traveled east, while the Black students traveled west.

Judge Duncan was appointed by President Nixon in 1974 as the first African American federal judge in Ohio. He had served as a Columbus prosecutor, an Ohio Supreme Court justice, and a judge on the US Military Court of Appeals. He was a Korean War veteran and a graduate of The Ohio State University Law School.

I don't think it is a coincidence that POER gathered the momentum at that time to file their class action lawsuit in the same court that had just endured the public outrage over desegregation. One of the staff attorneys working on the desegregation plan had even been shot in a federal courthouse by an angry citizen—it was a violent and contentious time in the Southern District of Ohio.

There had been previous lawsuits against the Columbus Division of Police under the Civil Rights Act. Some were successful, even though one that resulted from a particularly brutal attack on a Black couple celebrating a college graduation at the Kahiki restaurant was surprisingly thrown out by Judge Duncan. But the racial discrimination continued with the support of entrenched political officials and bureaucratic managers.

POER v. the City of Columbus took six years to come to trial. It was a bench trial, meaning no jury was seated and Judge Duncan was solely responsible for the verdict. POER called sixty witnesses over four weeks, and the city responded with thirty witnesses over two weeks. It took Judge Duncan almost a year to issue his decision. Even though he had been appointed to the bench for life, he retired in April of 1985, only three months after he issued this decision on January 8, 1985. He was fifty-seven. His writing in the decision reflected a tremendous amount of outrage and sadness.

In the trial, Chief Earl Burden (1972 - 1983) testified that Black officers were underrepresented in bureaus such as SWAT (Special Weapons and Tactics), Detective, and Traffic, and admitted that he had done nothing to change the practice. POER charged that the Columbus Division of Police discriminated against Black officers in the areas of promotions, assignments, transfers, and discipline. But the testimony went well beyond those claims, providing evidence of widespread hiring discrimination, personal threats and attacks on Black employees, illegal activity toward Black citizens, and other bigoted and racist behavior condoned by the leadership.

A particularly persuasive testimony was given by a white couple, Steve Brown and Sheila Bagley, who were both sworn Columbus officers. They had learned from Dr. Harry Topolosky, the doctor who conducted the physical examinations for acceptance to the academy, that he looked for any reason he could find to disqualify Black recruits. He expressed disappointment when he was unable to find anything wrong with them and therefore had to pass them on their physicals. Both officers reported this discovery, one to the chief and one to the civil service board, but nothing was done to discipline or replace Dr. Topolosky.

Another white officer, Sergeant Marion Ridge, testified that he actually resigned from the division in anger and frustration after trying to correct a discriminatory practice without success. He heard Lieutenant Richard Foor, the commander of the SWAT team, tell a Black officer in 1975 that as long as he was in charge, no "nigger" would serve on SWAT. When Ridge reported this to the chain of command, he was assured that the commander would be disciplined.

Instead the commander was promoted from lieutenant to captain at the recommendation of Chief Burden.

These white officers were not alone in their support of an equitable work environment. Throughout the history of civil rights struggles, there have been allies who have risked their jobs and safety to help move the effort forward. I work with many today as well, who see firsthand that we are not done eliminating systemic racism from this police department, but still have little power to change it.

On the other hand, there are Black officers caught in the mindset that going along with the system is the best way to get by. Four Black officers actually testified for the defense at the trial. One of them was Sergeant Stevens, my training officer at the academy. He testified that he had been offered a job with SWAT but turned it down because it didn't interest him. Other Black officers reported similar experiences and said they hadn't ever experienced racism themselves. All of this testimony—even if accurate—didn't add up to anything close to refuting the overwhelming evidence of entrenched systems of discrimination in hiring and assignments.

Officer Gary McCants, who is Black, testified for the plaintiffs that he had been assigned the job of spying on the leadership of the Black community, including the NAACP. He was frustrated because his investigation never exposed illegal activity and he felt like an intelligence officer spying on another country, but instead it was his own people. To be used like this by the white power structure is the essence of oppression. Did he have any status to request another assignment? Did they make him feel he was gaining status by doing this?

Hiring Black people to be police officers was a problem for Columbus. Especially when a good number of those who applied were being turned away by a bigoted physician for exaggerated or manufactured medical problems. At the time of Judge Duncan's decision in January of 1985, the population of the City of Columbus was 18.5 percent Black, while only 4 percent of the police department was Black. Title VII of the Civil Rights Act of 1964 was applied to municipal governments in 1972, prohibiting discrimination in hiring on the basis of sex, race, color, national origin, and religion. A previous decision in Haynie v. Chupka handed down in 1975 found that the city discriminated against Black applicants for the academy. It was clear from the evidence in this lawsuit that nothing much had changed — and more importantly, no one in power actually wanted it to change.

Along with systematically preventing Black citizens from becoming police officers, the Columbus Division of Police then segregated those they did hire from white officers in an overt and oppressive way. Conditions had improved somewhat since the first Black man was hired in 1895. There was a time when Black officers were not allowed to drive police vehicles and were only assigned to foot patrols. And then a time when we could drive, but we weren't allowed to have radios in our cars to communicate with dispatchers.

Well into the late 1960s, Black officers were never assigned to work in prisoner transport vehicles. One Black officer applying for that assignment was told, "We don't need no Sambos." This policy was so entrenched that if no white officers were available to staff the vans, the transport would be cancelled. Chief James Jackson (1990 - 2009), an African American who had plowed through the ranks to become a deputy chief at the time of the POER trial, testified that in 1969 he had questioned the refusal to integrate the wagons and was told by a captain that integration would only give you a "nigger and a hillbilly."

Almost all assignments for Black officers were in the patrol units in Black neighborhoods. A Black officer testified in the trial that he had never been paired with a white officer for patrol duty. When his partner was sick or on vacation, he would have no partner for the day and be forced to work by himself. White officers were never required to work alone. Some white officers specifically asked to be assigned Black partners, but one white officer testified that he was told in 1973 that if he continued to associate with Black officers he would go nowhere in the division.

The testimony of many veteran officers confirmed that these racist assignment policies had long-standing historical precedent. This is a culture that was born in the Reconstruction era, fit right into the Jim Crow era, and hadn't yet jumped on the Civil Rights–era bandwagon. The opportunities for assignment to special units were virtually nonexistent for Black officers. Just like SWAT, other divisions had been successful at selecting only white applicants for open assignments, with no scrutiny or fear of repercussions. For example, there were no Black detectives, except for specific positions assigned to look for stolen goods in pawnshops. Other units such as the Traffic Bureau and Training Bureau totally excluded Black applicants for many years. As of the date of the trial in 1984, no Black officer had worked in the Crime Scene Search Unit.

Even within the units that hired Black officers, the institutionalized discriminatory practices made advancement difficult. Statistical analysis was presented at the trial to prove that Black officers following all the rules and performing their duties with excellence would not be promoted, receive special assignments, or get preference in shifts at the same rate as white officers. Judge Duncan's ruling ordered that specific practices be eliminated or modified to create an equitable work environment.

Evidence at the trial confirmed that the sergeant's test had been specifically designed and graded to prevent Black officers from passing. As a result of Judge Duncan's decision, fifteen Black officers were promoted to sergeant in 1987, tripling the number of Black sergeants. One of them was my father-in-law, but he had to wait an uncharacteristic three years and go through additional screening and interviews to determine his suitability.

In its decision, the court also required that Black officers be reassigned to units where they had been denied entry in the past. But the court did not attempt to balance the ranks of lieutenant or captain, which were also underrepresented by Black officers. It concluded that the sergeants who were being installed by the court order could then pursue eventual promotions through "fair and nondiscriminatory" procedures. Only one of the fifteen promoted to sergeant that year advanced to lieutenant (and then on to commander) during his career, leaving us to wonder how "fair and nondiscriminatory" the procedures really were.

Even though the case was filed to prove equal employment discrimination, a majority of the trial was filled with evidence of a coordinated and supported culture of racial animus by white officers toward their Black coworkers. What appeared was a canvas of bullying, intimidation, hazing, and blatant disregard for the humanity of Black officers. Witness testimony recounted racial slurs, threats, and images on the desks at the training academy, bulletin boards, and restroom walls at various substations. There was overwhelming evidence exposing the frequent and unrestricted use of the word "nigger" in addition to other racially offensive terms and phrases.

Some white officers added what they might have felt was some creativity or humor to their bigoted behavior. One Black female officer testified that two white officers had presented her with a bunch of bananas in an attempt to label her a member of the ape family. One white captain welcomed a training class by reminding the cadets that while the division was required by law to accept Blacks and women into the academy, they were under no obligation to keep them. There was no evidence that behavior of this kind had ever been subject to disciplinary action or even discouraged.

Judge Duncan's discomfort was most evident in his acknowledgment that this behavior needed to be discussed in his judgment in order to explain the hostile conditions that Black officers endured to carry out their duties. It was apparent to him that it would be next to impossible for the Black officers to conduct themselves with the professionalism and dignity that all police officers are expected to display. The testimony that impacted the judge most was from Richard Leigh, a Black officer assigned in 1979 to the 8th Precinct, a poor area of Columbus just west of downtown commonly called "The Bottoms." The following happened a year after the case was filed, which tells us that no one in leadership was taking racism or the lawsuit seriously.

Leigh was often referred to as "token" or "Brillo pad" by his white coworkers. They delighted in a pattern of hazing by sending him on bogus calls. Once he responded to a suspicious person call only to discover a lawn jockey, one of the little Black boy statues historically displayed by homes along the underground railroad. Another time he was sent by himself to an open field near a cemetery to be confronted by six men in white sheets surrounding a burning cross. This was in 1979 in Columbus, Ohio.

The men in white sheets were police officers from his precinct. They said it was a "joke." Forty years later, it is unlikely that any of them are still with the division, but they continued to work until retirement and influenced the current culture.

In Judge Duncan's judgment, he ordered the Columbus Division of Police to increase its percentage of Black officers up to 18.5 percent, to match the percentage of Black residents in Columbus. Forty-five percent of each training class would need to be Black until that percentage was achieved. The last eight Black officers needed to reach this goal graduated from the academy in 1988. Linda, my first training officer, was in that class. The last ones still working with us will be retiring in October of 2022. Since the hiring mandate was lifted, Columbus has dwindled to under 11 percent minority officers while the population of Columbus is now 28 percent African American. The 192 Black officers working in 2018 are fewer than the Black officers hired from 1985 to 1988 to achieve initial parity.

With the victory in court in January of 1985, the officers who had joined POER returned to work with more worries than they had going in. They were now labeled as troublemakers and watched carefully. This led to a downturn in membership as officers were afraid to join POER for fear of being targeted. The organization is currently run by one of the fifteen sergeants promoted by the court order, even though he is now retired. They hold an annual Martin Luther King Day breakfast and have little influence inside the police department beyond the respect they receive from Black officers like myself.

The fight was not over as Duncan's successor, US District Judge James Graham, inherited a mess when three years later, POER and Columbus had not yet come to an agreement on how the order to increase Black representation in the department would be implemented. When they seemed to be getting close to an agreement, a group of white officers filed to be a party to the suit over the objections of both original parties. They claimed that any change in hiring and assignment practices that repaired the proven discrimination would now discriminate against the white officers. The judge allowed them to join the case.

Chief Dwight Joseph (1983 - 1990), working with Mayor Dana Rinehart, made public statements and ordered actions to comply with the court order. There had been 126 unique allegations of racism raised under oath in the trial. Joseph ordered the IAB to investigate each one of them.

Six officers were disciplined, including the ones who dressed up as KKK members and burned the cross and the ones who gave bananas to a Black officer. One hundred and twenty were not. This set a precedent that discouraged Black officers from complaining about racist behavior and policies that still continue today.

4

A LUNCH DATE GOES
VERY WRONG

Earning various degrees and following rules landed me in the Training Bureau, where I was never allowed to train and never got invited to lunch, until one day. And then I learned how to sue the city.

In 2000, I got a job in the Advanced Training Unit of the Training Bureau. This is where the police department holds continuing education classes for veteran officers who have been on the job for a while. The unit has responsibility for any new policies or best practices that we want to roll out across the division. They also manage the state-mandated courses for the continuing education requirements the officers have to fulfill. When policy makers are interested in an important topic, like school shootings, the Advanced Training Unit gets the request to follow any new guidelines, develop lesson plans, teach the courses, and train other facilitators. They create PowerPoints, tests, and any other tools a facilitator might need.

When I applied for that assignment, we had to take a written test and a public speaking test. For the written test, we wrote an essay on a certain topic that we should be able to easily explain. The public speaking test was a presentation about that topic to a group of people who would then grade us. Four people put in for the job, and two of us passed these tests. The other guy had more seniority than me but then decided he didn't want it, so I got the job. The Ohio Police Officer Training Academy (OPOTA) establishes the guidelines for the local divisions to follow. They require five years' experience in policing to be an instructor, and I had only been with the Columbus Division of Police for three years. Thankfully, I was able to use my military police experience to count toward the five years.

When I got the job, Columbus required that I complete the instructor development course offered by OPOTA, a state-mandated course for all instructors who would be teaching recruits, even though I would only be teaching in-service officers. So I became a certified peace officer training instructor for the State of Ohio.

Kevin Hanford, a lawyer at the time as well as a white sergeant, was the supervisor of the training unit when I came on board. There were three Black women instructors when I arrived, who had all been there long before Sergeant Hanford took over the unit. The other trainers were white men. Hanford started weeding out the Black female instructors with tactics like requiring us to stand at roll call, making us recite the pledge of allegiance at the flagpole, and telling us we couldn't have personal calls at our desks even though the white male officers took personal calls whenever and wherever they pleased. Generally he went out of his way to make the rules more uncomfortable for us than our white coworkers.

When he transferred out the first Black officer, he blamed it on the fact that she had been involved in an altercation with her husband off duty and had revised her statement on a police report she filed. He considered that as untruthfulness and something that would not be consistent with the high standard we are held to on and off duty. By 2001, the other two ended up leaving because they didn't want the harassment. They saw that in order to have a long career they would need to leave the unit. They have all since had successful careers with the division, assigned to many other positions, including teaching recruits.

I was the only Black woman left in his unit. He continued to select only white men for positions that opened up. Two of the new instructors who came into the unit around 2002 had been in my recruit class at the academy.

It is important to understand that Sergeant Hanford was a man with a license to practice law and the power to design training for the entire division, a job he held from 2000 to 2005, before he retired in 2006. His actions helped to set the tone for not just his unit but the entire division for many years. He was fully supported by the chain of command above him. He designed and fostered a culture of blatant discrimination and retaliation that continues until today.

In the training unit we all worked in one big room, each with a desk of our own. The sergeant would come in the room and give everyone lesson plans to review for grammatical errors and to study so they could teach them. But without fail, he wouldn't give me one. He wouldn't let me teach any of the courses.

There was a meeting room with windows and blinds next to the room with our desks. Often I could look through the blinds to see that he had scheduled a meeting with my unit without me. The sergeant would just invite people to join him at a certain time and never tell me. When they came out of these meetings, they would act as though excluding me from projects was perfectly normal. I don't remember attending any meetings that excluded anyone else. It was clear he was trying to make me uncomfortable enough to leave the unit.

The only thing I was assigned was working with the Citizen's Police Academy, a program where people from the community would attend a nine-week training course to learn about policing through ride-alongs, tours, classroom sessions, and community experiences. Since it was the only thing I was allowed to do, I put 110 percent of my effort into it. I realized that after the citizens graduated, there was nothing in place to keep them connected to the police department or each other.

In 2004, I created a 501(c)(3) nonprofit organization to fill this need called the Citizen's Police Academy Alumni Association. Members were involved in community projects and supporting the police department in various ways, including staffing the food tents at community events and bringing food baskets to the substations on Christmas.

We had a board, dues-paying members, T-shirts and decals, and a robust fundraising effort. We had an office at the police academy and were recognized by the chief. It survived for almost fifteen years, but after I was promoted to sergeant the person who took over didn't have the same passion for it. It was disbanded in 2018.

The Citizen's Police Academy assignment had little to do with what everyone else in the training unit worked on — I didn't develop lesson plans, write course material, teach the courses, train facilitators, or review the effectiveness of the trainings. This put me at a disadvantage. Most of the officers in the unit had the same amount of time on the job as me. Two of them were hired the exact same year. I was the only instructor with both a college degree and military experience, but that didn't matter to the sergeant. He seemed to only be able to see my skin color and gender.

I was also excluded from the day-to-day culture of my unit to the point that they never included me in outside activities or even invitations to lunch. Then on a cool sunny day in the fall of 2003, they surprised the heck out of me and invited me to lunch. At first I didn't want to go, but I quickly changed my mind thinking I might as well tag along, not wanting to give them one more excuse to exclude me.

So I followed them to the parking lot and told Rich, an officer I had known since the academy, that I was coming along. He was in the driver's seat. I walked around his car and reached for the rear passenger door handle. As I started to open the door, Rich drove off with Scott and Brad, other officers in my unit. My hand released from the handle while I watched them all drive away. They didn't come back. They just left me standing there.

I finally said, "Enough." I went to Melvin Richardson, the equal employment officer for the City of Columbus, who recommended that I proceed informally with my complaint. He sent a letter to the commander of the training unit asking why I wasn't being given training assignments per my job description. When I went back to my desk I could sense that Sergeant Hanford already knew I had contacted the EEO office.

He called me into his office to discuss a Citizen's Police Academy matter. Earlier that week I had picked up a print job at the photo lab when a clerk was rude to me during a disagreement over how long the job was taking, and I had gotten smart right back. This clerk wrote a long complaint to my sergeant. Sergeant Hanford asked me why I had acted that way and immediately began chastising me. I complained that he didn't stop to listen to my side of the story. He looked directly at me and replied, "I don't give a fuck what you have to say."

Then he asked if I wanted to start accepting training assignments now, as if I hadn't wanted to in the past. At that moment it was clear to me that he knew that I had been to see the EEO officer, and that the EEO officer's recommendation to handle it informally was not going to work.

First, I filed a complaint against Sergeant Hanford. He was written up for swearing at me, which is against the rules. He received a DCC (documented constructive counseling), the lowest level of discipline that would only remain on his record for nine months. He admitted to the inappropriate speech because he thought I was recording him. He knew that admitting to swearing would get him less punishment than getting caught lying about it. There is an understanding that the Columbus Division of Police maintains a "liar's list," and there are certain jobs in the department you are not allowed to do if you are on the list, including working in the training unit. I hadn't recorded the interaction, but he didn't know that, and he didn't want to take a chance. He was very upset about the write-up and went home for the rest of the day, saying he had a dark cloud over his head. It seemed he fell out of favor with the chief after that.

Sergeant Hanford eventually was caught lying about another matter involving the ethics of a test he had developed and was consequently banned from the Training Bureau for the rest of his career. He retired on disability after that investigation.

Next I went back to Mr. Richardson to ask to file a formal complaint, and he told me they wouldn't do that for me. It seemed like his job was to squelch complaints and protect the city from liability. I only wanted to work under the same conditions as my white male counterparts. I wasn't asking for any special treatment, just to be given the same chance to do a good job.

On November 21, 2003, I filed a complaint with the US Equal Employment Opportunity Commission (EEOC) (Charge Number 224-2004-00588) against the City of Columbus. I hired a lawyer who helped me draft the complaint that describes the actions they took that were discriminatory against me, based on my race and gender.

The commission then sent the complaint to the city officials, who had a certain number of days to respond.

Sergeant Hanford answered the complaint by saying that I had told him that I didn't want to train, which was not true at all and made no sense. Why would I have applied for a training job, completed the additional state certification, and stayed there through all the harassment if I didn't want to be a trainer?

Maybe illogical excuses for discrimination had worked for him in the past, or maybe he had never had to explain himself to anyone inside this culture of rampant white male superiority. The Black female officers who left before me had not filed any complaints, to my knowledge—it was always easier and safer to just quietly move on and try to find an assignment where harassment was at a minimum.

I decided to stay and fight because I knew that if I allowed this sergeant to harass me to the point where I left the unit, it would affect the next Black woman who wanted to work in training. I knew how hard the officers before me had worked to give me the opportunity to be here, and I refused to be pushed out of a position I had a right to have. I also knew that if I ran at that point, I would be running for the rest of my career.

The EEOC conducted an investigation, interviewing various parties and requesting relevant documents. This process took almost five months. Surprisingly, my job description and my assignments remained the same throughout. In fact, during this time I was pulling together the new alumni association and working harder than ever on the Citizen's Police Academy.

After their investigation, the EEOC issued a determination on April 20, 2004, which found reason to believe that I was denied equal terms and conditions of employment and was discriminated against when I complained about discriminatory treatment, all in violation of Title VII of the 1964 Civil Rights Act. On May 18, 2004, the charge was referred to the US Department of Justice (DOJ) for review to determine what further action the DOJ would take.

When I opened the letter I felt relieved and overjoyed, but totally exhausted! It felt like all the sleepless nights and the retaliation I had endured was not in vain. Someone else, an outside agency, looked at the evidence and saw what I saw. It was validating.

While it was great to have an official governmental decision acknowledging what I already knew, it didn't change anything for the better. I had spent six months on paperwork, attorney meetings, hearings, research, and all of this was off the clock. It seemed that the EEOC had forgotten to copy the Columbus Division of Police on their decision. Or maybe Columbus did get it and just saw it as more reason to retaliate against me. In fact, things got even worse.

As I was navigating the EEO complaint process and the lawsuit, I was subjected to an even more hostile work environment. Retaliation was immediate and harsh. Sergeant Hanford put me on third shift from 11 p.m. to 7 a.m. for three weeks. I was isolated and treated more unfairly. He even opened my mail—a greeting card from a citizen—probably looking to see if I violated the rule against receiving personal mail at work.

At this point, it was clear to me that the EEOC had little power and put even less fear into the division. On October 1, 2004, I withdrew from the EEOC process and requested a right-to-sue letter to pursue my claim in federal court. I got an employment rights attorney, Charles McKinney.

On October 25, 2004, the EEOC issued a notice of right-to-sue letter advising me that I had ninety days to file a complaint with a federal court. Five days earlier, Sergeant Hanford, who was still my supervisor at the training unit, filed a complaint against me in the Franklin County Common Pleas Court, alleging that I defamed him when I made the allegations in the EEO complaint. This civil case was filed to retaliate against me and intimidate me from filing my case in the federal court. His case was dropped eventually as a condition of my settlement with the city. Not knowing my rights and having a marginally competent attorney, I didn't know that I should have filed another complaint against him for filing a frivolous lawsuit against me for participating in protected activity.

We filed on January 26, 2005 in the US District Court of Southern Ohio against the City of Columbus and Hanford. That day began twenty-seven months of legal proceedings that really opened my eyes to what the words "equal employment opportunity" can mean: I had an opportunity to be continuously harassed. I had an opportunity to be stressed and distracted from my everyday life. I had an opportunity to spend a great deal of my own money. Before it was all over, I had spent $30,000.

While representing me, McKinney missed several deadlines, resulting in the court sanctioning him with a fine of $1,500. These missed deadlines were factors in me losing my case through a motion for summary judgment. As I was planning an appeal, the city offered me a settlement that included a clause stating the city would not enforce the $1,500 sanction against McKinney. I had another attorney look at the case who told me there was nothing I could do, so I settled with the city on May 1, 2007.

Then I filed a complaint against McKinney with the Columbus Bar Association. We had a hearing, and I was awarded $11,000 of my attorney fees back. I collected $1,000 from him before he stopped paying. Another lawsuit resulted in a judgment against him. So I hired more attorneys to collect my judgment. To date, I have received only $3,000 from McKinney.

This entire process was such a hard thing to go through because everyone was against me. They made me feel like public enemy number one at the time, which I clearly wasn't. There is a culture in the police department of shunning anyone who files an EEO complaint. Everyone looked at me differently, and no one trusted me. People stopped talking to me, as though I was contagious. Even Black officers didn't want to associate publicly with me.

When an EEO complaint is filed, the IAB also conducts their own internal investigation to discover if any misconduct has occurred. Rich said he was just joking with me and that he turned around and came back and got me, which was not true at all. This IAB investigation was a joke because when a complaint is EEO related, they put little effort into it and never find fault with the person that discriminates. That practice continues today.

Not only did I sue the city, but I sued my coworkers in the training unit as well for conspiracy to violate my civil rights. I knew there would be no internal discipline handed down for their actions. They obviously didn't like this, but I wanted to make a point that they contributed to the mistreatment that I received. Even though the case did not result in any monetary remedies, it served its purpose to show them that I wouldn't tolerate discrimination.

The silly stuff that they enjoyed doing to make me uncomfortable happened all the time. Once they put a dummy in a chair with a bra on it. Some of the officers would make an effort to fart loudly when I was near them. They found very nasty and creative stuff to do just to inconvenience me and make me upset. One officer in the unit even sent an e-mail to everyone in the unit including me with a link to an article that stated workers don't need to associate with people they work with. After four years in the military working alongside very professional and ethical airmen, suddenly I was back in an elementary school culture where bullying was the norm, to establish a pecking order to feel better about oneself.

Having come from a tiny community, I wasn't used to running away from my problems. There was nowhere to go. My mother raised me not to start trouble but to stand up for myself if it comes my way. I would feel ashamed of myself if I didn't fight for myself. To put it simply, I'm just built this way.

— 5 —

WHAT MY TRAINING
OFFICER DIDN'T TELL ME

Navigating the union allegiances, the inner circle networks, and the outright bigots became a second full-time job that didn't come with a training manual.

In the military there were the rules, and there were ways to follow the rules. At the Columbus Division of Police there are the rules, and there are the ways around the rules. In the police academy and in my training phases that followed, I was taught those rules. Sometime after my training was over, I began to piece together how people got around the rules and still do.

As a woman and a Black person, I'm sure I wasn't really supposed to figure this out, or if I did I was expected to keep quiet about it. Many Black and women officers choose to not make waves and not challenge the entrenched system of corruption and racism. It is an effective job security strategy, but it puts us in a terrible position, leading to stress and personal turmoil.

My first lawsuit established me as someone willing to call out the established discriminatory practices. My reputation was building as a deeper thorn in the side of the status quo. Because of this, many officers came to me for advice on their most difficult situations. Even with all I know, there are still situations that I can't call out because it would harm innocent officers caught in the crossfire. I want to make clear that the thin black line is not a line where we are on one side or the other; it is a tightrope we have to balance on. Either side of it can bring career-ending consequences.

Much of this struggle is born in the lack of access to equal employment opportunity as we chart out our career as police officers. As Black officers, we quickly learn that we can't advance through the ranks and get the best assignments by following the same rules that work for white officers. We are always on edge, watching out for how we might be tripped up. As we begin to understand that we will never beat the system, we can become demoralized and defeated. These are not the attributes the community needs to foster in their police officers.

Let's start unpacking this with a quick view of the Fraternal Order of Police (FOP). The FOP Capital City Lodge #9 is one of 175 local groups that make up the FOP of Ohio with its 25,000 members. It's a union of sworn police department employees, with the stated mission of supporting the "social welfare of policing." Founded in 1920 in Canton, Ohio, after the first lodge began five years earlier across the Ohio River in Allegheny County, Pennsylvania, Ohio's FOP continues to be one of the most robust statewide organizations advocating for the working conditions of police officers. Our local lodge has more than 4,000 members and represents twenty-nine law enforcement agencies in and around Columbus, Ohio. Police and teachers unions are the largest faction of organized labor in the country, helping local governments to have the most unionized workforces of all employers.

The challenge for me and many officers of color is that, as an organization founded at the height of the Jim Crow era, the FOP did not historically consider the working conditions of Black (and also female) officers a concern. That culture lingers today. Certainly, many of the demands that they have bargained for and won in our contract, like pay rates, apply equally to everyone. Others are only there on the surface. Digging deeper into what actually happens, it becomes obvious that these contractual protections are not applied uniformly across gender and race lines.

Unsurprisingly, the leadership of the FOP itself has skewed white and male. Even the lead picture on the Ohio FOP website today in 2020 shows not much diversity among forty or fifty officers, with only four Black men and one white woman among them. They are not even pretending to encourage a diversified workforce or work toward recruiting diverse leadership.

The POER lawsuit documented a variety of ways that the FOP was not engaged in protecting their members of color. In the wake of the Duncan decision in 1985, Columbus was mandated to assign a certain number of minority officers to nonpatrol assignments. When most people think of the police, patrol officers usually come to mind, because those are the ones they see every day out in the streets. But a police department functions with a wide variety of assignments, and most of the more desirable ones are not in the Patrol Bureau. Our pay rate is determined by rank, so the assignment we have adds or detracts significantly from our job satisfaction. In fact, being returned to a patrol assignment is used as a punishment if you get in trouble in a nonpatrol job.

The first three years in the division, we are officers. Then we can test to become a sergeant. Each rank above that is achieved by passing a standard test that grades us on our ability to do the tasks at that rank. With each advancement in rank, we receive a contractually negotiated pay bump.

Every open assignment is posted on the daily bulletin, sent out in a division-wide e-mail. Everyone has access to it, and anyone can apply to the open positions for their rank. After applications are received, they are organized by the amount of time each applicant has worked at that rank. On the surface at least, that looks like a pretty good system for eliminating racism or sexism.

To fulfill the new legal requirements from the Duncan decision, a listing might have stated that they need a Black woman. This requirement was lifted around 2002 because the current procedures are supposed to be designed to enforce parity for nonpatrol assignments. But the process has snapped back to preference for white men. They come up with very clever ways to pass over minorities without breaking the stated rules, or sometimes just break them outright.

One well-worn way to do this was to list exceptional qualifications for an assignment. If a supervisor wanted to give it to a specific person who they knew would be far down the list sorted by seniority, they could find out in advance what exceptional qualifications their preferred candidate has, like a bachelor's degree in criminal justice for example, that others might not have. Then they can request an exceptional qualification be attached to the job assignment, allowing them to ignore the seniority rule and pick whomever they want who has that specific qualification.

I watched this strategy work seamlessly a few years ago when there were two openings for recruit training positions at the police academy. If a job has exceptional qualifications, they are automatically listed when posted. After several dozen candidates submitted applications, the list of applicants was sorted by seniority. The first on the list was a white man, who was offered the position. A Black female was now first on the seniority list for the second position. The sergeant decided to go by the exceptional qualifications and skipped down the list to number forty-five to pick a white female, who some believed to be a friend of the chief. There were a lot of white and Black officers skipped over, so the intent was clearly not a racial preference, but this type of rule bending resulted in many lost opportunities for Black officers.

Rather than embrace the opportunity to have diverse trainers, this action left the recruit training academy with no Black female training officers—a critical mistake for a department that was previously mandated to attract and retain minority officers. The impression that the new recruits get at the academy forms a basis for their expectations of the culture in the division. It also instills the respect that they are expected to show to minorities, both on the job and in the community.

The Black woman who had been number one on the list and was eager to work in the academy filed a grievance through the union. To resolve the grievance and prevent a lawsuit, the division offered her the next opening for the position. With no assurance of when that would be, and quite sure she would be working with people that clearly did not want her working there, she turned down the offer. But she made her point, exposed the discriminatory practice, and changed the system. Any jobs that are filled now by exceptional qualifications must also go in order of seniority.

A prestigious path to advancement within the Columbus Division of Police is to apply for special task forces. They are created to partner with another law enforcement agency, possibly at the state or federal level. Designed to attack a specific crime problem or look for a crime prevention solution, they can have different time frames but are currently staffed for five-year terms.

Officers enjoy these assignments for several reasons. Often they come with better hours, at new locations, working out of uniform while doing more interesting tasks and learning new skills. We are exposed to the tactics used by the different agencies and work with federal agents to pool resources. The assignments truly enhance an officer's skill set and are considered to be distinguished jobs.

When an agency, like DEA or ATF, asks for Columbus officers to join a local task force operation, a sergeant is assigned to lead the division involvement. These sergeants have always been white men. Then that sergeant handpicks the officers to serve with him, routinely picking his friends, and—no surprise—those friends are almost always white men. It's a little like joining a secret club within a fraternity. The first time a Black man was selected for any task force that I'm aware of was in 2016, thirty years after the Duncan decision. The first woman was selected a year before that, but she happened to be the wife of a deputy chief. She was as qualified as any good officer for that assignment, but she was part of that inner circle who could crash through that barrier.

Women have another problem in qualifying for some assignments. There are physical tests designed specifically so that women cannot pass them, due to upper body strength requirements. The test for SWAT is one of them—I don't recall any women ever having been assigned to SWAT during my career. Some tests require advanced math skills, public speaking skills, and other skills that are not required or relevant for a specific job—every hoop to jump through to get desirable assignments favors white men.

Another way Black and women officers are kept from qualifying for assignments is a practice called "sixty-day temps." These temporary assignments offer officers opportunities to gain valuable experience. They might offer an officer an assignment involving undercover work, or special tactics, or managerial processes, to give us some insight into the work and learn if we would like to pursue that career path.

There is no way to get in line for these temp assignments, because they always go to the friends of the ranking officers who staff the positions. There is an assumption that they just know who will be good at one type of position or another, so they pigeonhole us into tracks. You can see how easy it is for the established white male leadership to continue to select other white men for the best temporary assignments if no one tells them they can't.

A significant exception to this rule is the sixty-day temp requests for attractive women. The sergeants are happy to have new cute officers, while passing up more senior but less physically attractive officers. I know that these younger officers have the same qualifications and are just as hardworking—they do not ask for and probably do not want this advantage on the job. It creates a special form of exploitation when the male officers know the women were selected only for their appearance.

This leaves women and minorities unable to "qualify" for assignments solely based on friendships with those staffing the positions. I should also mention that not all white men make the cut either—some are never favored for reasons I can't begin to imagine. And occasionally a Black man is accepted into the inner circle to help with the optics, but then he has to work very hard to get along with the inner circle and pay back this favor.

It's also hard to get into the line for leadership courses. Officers are picked for these courses based on favoritism, so women and minorities rarely get a spot. Many of these courses are required as a prerequisite when we apply for a leadership or chief position in another police department. I don't have any problem with making this type of training a requirement for specific assignments, but the problem is they are not open to everyone and therefore are used as a tool for discrimination. I personally tried to get into a specific leadership course and was turned down twice. Then I watched officers with less seniority than me get approval to attend. It is about favoritism. I have discovered what it is like to not be the favorite.

Interviews are not part of the assignment process unless it states so in the posting. Most are only posted with the rank and any exceptional qualifications. All officers that apply are listed in order by seniority, which is how long they have been with the division. If the top person on the list wants the job, it is supposed to be theirs. But if the supervisor doesn't like that person, they might call them in for an interview. The "interview" is just an opportunity for the supervisor to tell the person entitled to the assignment all the reasons they will not want the job. These can include all the ways the supervisor will make the job undesirable for them, like scheduling them at difficult hours. Sometimes there is a concerted effort where all the officers in the unit call an applicant to talk them out of it. Once this starts happening, the applicant knows they aren't wanted and would be walking into a toxic work environment, so they turn down the assignment.

I saw these discriminatory processes early in my career and knew that my advancement within the division would depend on my achievement outside the division. Yet my ongoing higher education and the degrees I have earned are still ignored when it is convenient to exclude me. It's like the straight A kid being the last to be picked for dodgeball. You might assume a police department would operate with slightly more sophisticated criteria than what we used in sixth grade to pick our friends for playground games, but that's what the assignment process feels like. It is discouraging and it often makes people angry.

All minority officers working at the Columbus Division of Police who are hoping to get the better assignments notice these blatant discrimination tactics. In a perfect world, everyone should be encouraged to work in any position where they are qualified. The division invests a lot in training and then wastes that money by stifling or sidelining some of the best officers. We are passed over for positions we are qualified for and have the seniority to achieve. It is demoralizing to officers who see that no matter how well we do our job, or how long we work and what qualifications we attain, we can still be passed over because of race or gender.

It has been fifty years since Title VII made this practice illegal. But like many laws designed to eliminate racism and sexism, organizations just got better at hiding it. These illegal actions change career paths and lives of dedicated officers, sometimes to the point that they leave our department or policing entirely. Understanding this, it is not hard to see why we have the problem we do retaining minority officers.

Assignments matter. They are the stepping-stones that officers take to becoming better officers, feeling proud of our careers, and interacting well with the community. It is not just about fairness; it is about having an effective police department where everyone operates at peak performance. It's basic human resource management. But instead we have a culture where discrimination against minorities is institutionalized and encouraged. That mindset carries over into our relationship with the community we serve in Columbus, 40 percent of whom are people of color and over half are women.

This pattern of circumventing seniority as the criteria that will eliminate discrimination extends all the way to the top and applies to the most senior positions. In June of 2019, I was a lieutenant working Sunday through Thursday on the second shift from 3 p.m. to 11 p.m.—the busiest shift—supervising the largest zone in the city with the most patrol calls for service. Zone 2 is at the far southeast end of the city with a culturally and economically diverse population. It is a thriving area with a variety of residential, commercial, and industrial areas to patrol. A new position I am qualified for was posted called watch commander. This position would have chief authority to handle disputes between bureaus and keep the chief informed during the second and third shifts when he is not at work. There were two openings on each shift. I applied for all four.

Chief Thomas Quinlan (2019 - present) had filled the two second-shift positions with white men he liked immediately after he posted them. He did not call me to see if I wanted either one of those openings. On the list for the third-shift position, I was number one when ranked by seniority. The chief called me, saying he was contacting me to see if I was interested. I asked, "Are you offering me the job?" He responded that he was not. He was going through the entire list to see who wanted it. I challenged him that he had not done that for the second-shift positions because I would have been called. But then, when I am the top candidate on a list, he has to call everyone for some reason.

He explained he felt justified in his right to choose whomever he wanted because he needed someone who would represent his interests. He said he could pass me over, even though he knew it was a seniority-based assignment. In fact, the first thing he said was, "There will probably be a grievance filed on this." I replied, "You are telling me that you are probably going to skip me and pick someone with less seniority. That will be embarrassing." He disagreed and replied, "Not for me; we do this all the time."

A long conversation followed, during which he told me how closely he had worked with other people on the list over the years. So, because of all the reasons I have shared here about assignments, I had not had the same opportunities to work with him as other officers on the list had — my seniority advantage did not matter. I was thinking of a recent e-mail he had sent to everyone stating that he picked people for assignments who had a reputation for getting things done. So it didn't matter how long I had worked or how well I did my job or what the union contract said—I was not a white male. He was not at all afraid of any grievance I would file knowing the union does not support minority officers in EEO complaints.

In January of 2020, I applied for another assignment as the discipline/grievance supervisor. For the last seven years, this job had been filled based on the exceptional qualification of a law degree, which by that point I had. Instead of giving me the job because I was the most senior person with the exceptional qualification, he chose to fill the job based on seniority and gave the job to a white male without a law degree. So when I had the seniority but not the degree, he would not offer me the job; when I had the exceptional qualification for the job, he went by seniority. Both times the job went to less qualified white males, based on years of service, experience, and education. There is no way to win if they do not want me in a job. They always find a way around the rules, especially if they know when I file a grievance the union will not stand behind me.

After the tremendous effort from the POER lawsuit and other actions of Black officers over the last one hundred years, there was a moment when it looked like we were making progress right around the time I came into the department in the late 1990s. When I look around today and see all the stress and frustration from women and Black officers, it seems like we are heading right back to the same conditions of the mid-twentieth century where Black officers were only allowed to have certain segregated assignments and female officers were corralled into certain jobs that were "suitable" for women. When the chief is leading with this type of bigoted decision-making, everyone down the line sees that this is the way we do things, and the Columbus Division of Police's legacy of discrimination continues.

HOW TO BE A COP IN THE BLACK LIVES MATTER ERA

#BlackLivesMatter made it more important for cops to be "blue," but I'm still Black, which adds to the stress and danger of the job.

The phrase "thin blue line" has a long history dating back to the Crimean War, and was originally used to mean the line that police walk between the citizens and anarchy. Somewhere along the way, its meaning changed to imply the secrets that cops keep behind the line and the "blue code of silence" we uphold to keep those secrets. This was a bad thing when I became an officer. We denied that there was such a code—we certainly denied that we covered for each other's lies. Even though we did. And still do.

When the hashtag #blacklivesmatter was launched in 2013 after the acquittal of George Zimmerman in the Trayvon Martin killing in Florida, things slowly started to change.

Counter hashtags emerged that included #bluelivesmatter. People even made us #bluelivesmatter signs for our precincts. These two phrases became polar opposites in some people's minds—in the Columbus Division of Police, it solidified the notion that we are walking a thin blue line to defend ourselves against how people think we treat the Black community.

As a police officer, I could never use the phrase "Black Lives Matter" freely. The police culture around me categorized the social media movement as a terrorist organization. Until white people started to use the phrase, Black people had to stay silent.

The first time I noticed this shift was in the summer of 2016. Henry Green, a twenty-three-year-old Black man, was shot and killed in the Linden area of Columbus by plainclothes officers. The officers were not following protocol when they confronted Green out of uniform. I often wonder if the result would have been different if the officers had called for a marked cruiser to approach. The predominantly Black community of Linden was shocked and outraged. Even though we had recently had a training on social media usage to make sure we didn't show the division in a bad light, several officers in a police Facebook group discussed a protest event they found on Facebook called #BlackLivesMatter—Columbus, saying they expected it to be violent. Several officers offered messages of safety, but others took it up a notch:

"We should meet them and talk to them, hear them out, listen and understand . . . :)"

"I hope your (sic) going out in full riot gear, this bullshit not wearing it to look peaceful is ridiculous. Be prepared."

"Bring it mother fuc*ers!!! Bring it!"

"Seriously we need to start watching our six."

And then they crossed a line:

 Trent Taylor
Anybody know where I can get some C-4???
6 hours ago · 👍 1

 Matt David
Military taught me how to make my own stuff to go boom. C4 is great though.
5 hours ago · 👍 1

The mention of C-4, a plastic explosive, by Sergeant Trent Taylor with the follow-up comment that flaunts bomb-making skills entered the realm of a terrorist threat. At the very least, it was unprofessional behavior. A Black officer saw this post and was afraid of retaliation if he reported it himself. So he sent it to a Black dispatcher who wrote a letter requesting an investigation and sent it to her chain of command, who then referred it to IAB, who then ruled that the C-4 comment was a joke. So the officers had no discipline meted out for their conduct. But in predictable fashion, the dispatcher experienced retaliation for reporting it.

Just recently during the 2020 protests, Sergeant Taylor retired due to the Black Lives Matter protests. He shared during an interview on a local television station that officers are now forced to retire due to the way citizens are demanding that the police change the way they treat Black lives. This calls into question this officer's entire career and how deep-rooted his hatred of Black people is.

As Sergeant Taylor's investigation was going on, I attended roll calls to express to my personnel that they needed to be careful what they post on social media. I told them that I might believe that Black lives matter, and they might believe that blue lives matter. Everyone is entitled to their opinion, and it's not worth getting in trouble over an argument on social media. I had one officer that wanted to argue with me about using that example. I immediately shut him down and went on to another topic. This conversation came up at a later IAB investigation on me, implying I had raised the flag for the enemy that day when all I was trying to do was keep everyone out of trouble on social media.

The transition is now complete. We are "blue." We wave an American flag with a blue line through it, and the FOP distributed blue wristbands that some officers have worn while in uniform. We think of ourselves as different. Even Black and female officers can get caught up in it. I have to check myself sometimes because it is a highly coercive culture, not too dissimilar from a gang or a cult.

It starts in the police academy. When we enter they tell us we will change, our friends will change, and our family will tell us that we've changed. We learn about the high divorce rate among officers. A representative comes out from the academy to talk to our families about the changes we will go through. We will not like crowds, we'll never sit with our backs to the door, and we'll be very antisocial when we come home each day.

But instead of offering us wellness programs to help us adjust, they brainwash us and our families into simply accepting this different behavior that sets us apart from normal people. It lays the foundation of the notion that we are not only different, but we are better.

We end up with a culture of elitism. We have set ourselves so far apart that we believe no one can understand us— not the residents we serve or the politicians we report to. The badge and the gun make us special. This is a totally different mindset than what I learned in the military. The law enforcement officers in the military were no better or worse than the people we served. I'm still not used to the prevailing culture in the police department, and it rubs up against my values every day.

We trick ourselves into believing that the rest of the population can't relate to us because they can't walk in our shoes. It takes a special person to do what we do. The minimum education requirement to enter the academy has been a GED (General Education Development test), so some officers arrive with low self-esteem issues. This indoctrination pumps us up to feel superior to the people we serve, to overcompensate for any feelings of inadequacy we may have. It is easy to buy into the notion that we are more important than we are and part of an elite force.

Officers also develop an "us vs. them" mentality. We learn that we are warriors with a warrior spirit, or we are the sheepdogs and everyone else is sheep, or they are victims walking around clueless and it is our job to protect them. We like to remind ourselves that we are the ones who run toward gunfire when everyone else runs away. However we frame it, we thrive on being in a class by ourselves. Our nickname is "Columbus's Finest."

The public began to buy into this. We have stars on the backs of our personal cars signifying that we are police. We have "get out of jail free" cards we give to our family members. We get free food at restaurants and free coffee at convenience stores.

Society is not helping by putting us on this pedestal. I know there are citizens who sincerely appreciate what we do and want to thank us. But this divide between the division and the community spills over into our own house. The Columbus Division of Police is still dominated by a fraternity of white men who find it difficult to treat people of color and women inside the division with equal respect—they find it hard to swallow that we are blue too.

Much of this culture is reinforced outside of our walls at the union level. With 1,900 officers in Columbus, we make up almost half of the membership of our local FOP lodge which includes agencies from around Franklin County. I was having lunch recently with a very active white male member of the union. What turned into a three-hour conversation helped me understand more of how this culture is reinforced.

At first he denied ever seeing any incidents of excessive force used against people of color. He joined the profession to help people, as many of us did, but has not yet developed any empathy for the plight of people who do not look like him.

But the longer we talked, the more he recognized that he actually has seen some patterns of behavior, like officers who get mad when a suspect runs and then use their taser to punish them. Police reports of incidents do not always accurately reflect the order that events occurred. For example, a suspect might throw a punch in response to being tased. But the written report would say the punch happened first.

That strategy is born out of a strong desire to protect officers at all costs. The very active FOP member condones certain behaviors that are clearly unauthorized actions by police—he has aspirations to go higher in the union, so he has to protect all officers, right or wrong. He is using his power to protect bad officers. That is his job.

Each Black officer and each woman has to decide for themselves how to get along with the culture. Members of oppressed classes have always had this challenge. Different strategies work for different people. My confrontational strategy of overt resistance from the start, on my own, is not normal today. Certainly POER was a group formed to eliminate the risk that each officer faced when acting on their own. But even after a ten-year federal lawsuit that they won, they were eventually defeated by retaliation and unending racism.

Some Black officers choose to adopt the culture of white supremacy over the Black community themselves, and use tactics that go beyond policy boundaries and inflict harm. A case that became very public because of a viral video was that of Anthony Johnson, a Black officer who had worked for me as an officer when I was the second-shift lieutenant in Zone 2. This was an area that was so understaffed that officers needed to be efficient to respond to all our waiting calls. There were a few neighborhoods that didn't trust the police, but for the most part people called when they needed help.

Johnson had three incidents in five months where he had punched a suspect in the face. Each of the incidents were investigated and found to be within policy. In this culture, this is not surprising. Most use-of-force incidents are found to be within policy. For the rare ones that are not, the officer receives very little discipline, if any at all.

Since Officer Johnson had significantly more uses of force involving striking a person than most officers, I called him into my office with his sergeant for a meeting. I explained to him that I understood that all of his punches were found in policy, but I was concerned that he was not using lower levels of force but instead was starting off punching people. I told him just because he can strike a person doesn't mean he always should.

He transferred to Zone 5 shortly after our conversation, where a lot of officers who enjoy the adrenaline rush choose to work. Many Black residents there do not trust the police, so they don't call in for help. That leaves the officers free to self-initiate activity. I called his new lieutenant and told him I had an issue with him punching people in the face.

One night a couple of years later, I turned on the news and there was Johnson throwing a punch. The man he hit had been asked to leave his house where his children were because a "shot spotter" had gone off in the neighborhood. Shot spotters are microphones that are placed on the top of buildings to detect the sounds of gunshots. The police agency is sent an immediate alert and is able to have units on the way, likely before the first phone call comes in.

The man had been yelling at another officer to let his wife go back in to get their children. The officer told him to back up or he would be arrested. I could tell by their behavior that the other officers in the immediate area did not feel threatened. No one had their gun out. They were just milling around waiting for the call to be over. They had already determined no one in the neighborhood had been shot.

Then seemingly out of nowhere, Johnson came running toward the father with his shotgun across his chest and pushed him back. Then he took another step forward, and he threw a punch to the father's face.

The division found that this punch was within policy. But again, that is not surprising. My recommendation would have found him out of policy because the officer had to step toward the male in order to strike him, showing there was no immediate threat. And the father was not being placed under arrest. We have a culture that would say the father deserved to be punched for yelling and looking like he was squaring up on the officer.

I spoke with his lieutenant after watching the video and was told that Johnson had punched two people when he started working in Zone 5. His lieutenant had a talk with him, and he hadn't punched anyone for two years until the video.

When a cell phone video captures bad behavior, the chances are very high that it isn't the first time the officer caught in the act has misbehaved that way. None of the news stories I saw about this incident brought up this officer's past use of force, even though they could have easily asked for records of any previous investigations into his conduct. Even then, those actions fall off our records after a few years. The fact that he was caught on video this time might be enough to get him to stop throwing punches, but he is not mandated to get counseling or training or anything that might help him do his job better in the future. All he gets is affirmation that he won't be disciplined if he does it again. Everyone knows that, and the lack of consequences for bad behavior perpetuates the brutality.

There were thirty-nine disciplinary cases from 2015 to the beginning of 2020 that were egregious enough to have to go in front of the chief. Two received a written reprimand, which is a write-up that stays in their file for three years. One case involved an officer striking a suspect in the head with a flashlight, and the other involved an officer kicking a suspect in the butt twice. Using force on citizens is rarely punished, and when it is punished the punishments are hardy ever significant.

The invention of video cameras embedded in cell phones changed the public's perception of policing forever. Body-worn cameras (BWCs) have done even more, because they are supposed to be on all the time during police encounters with citizens. BWCs were one of the first successful demands of Black Lives Matter activists. They knew that citizens' versions of police behavior were very different from the reports generated by police themselves and thought cameras would fix that.

I love the BWCs because they allow us to see much of the officer's behavior. The union demanded that the officer be allowed to review the footage before they make a statement or write a report. You can be sure officers will not volunteer any information that would reflect poorly on themselves if it's not proven through the video. If they have done something inappropriate, they will be able to figure out how much they need to admit to, and no more—it's more important to be consistent with the body camera than to be truthful about what happened.

I remember an arrest for car theft where the officer did a very bad job articulating his bad judgment. He used unnecessary force and blamed it on the fear that the driver of the stolen car would back up into him.

The hole in his story was that he parked around the corner, away from the stolen car, and prepared the weapons before he even saw exactly where the stolen car was. He busted the car window and pepper-sprayed both people inside. The suspects were subjected to excessive force. The officer thought he could get away with it, his sergeant decided he was "in policy," and it took us a minute to get to the truth, wasting everyone's time. But we had the BWC footage, which did not show acceptable conditions for his actions. Without that, it would have been easy to believe the officer's story.

They have not fixed everything, of course, but BWCs have helped to diminish serious police brutality. Some officers forget they are wearing one, amazingly, and still act badly. Others change their behavior when they know someone is watching. I have experienced this my entire career as the sergeant, and then lieutenant, who would follow the book and correct officers when they did not.

I know bad behaviors change when I walk in the room. When I can't see what is happening, maybe a body camera will catch it. If that fails, I know that God sees all and will try to protect the victims of police brutality.

I know by just being in the police department, I deter things from happening to Black and poor people. Most of the officers don't come from the same oppressed culture and have no empathy for how these people came to be where they are in life. Police develop the mindset that people in the community deserve the abuse they get. It has been scary for me to witness this and try to speak out against the culture when I can. But it's even scarier to think about what it would look like if I were not here.

7

IT'S HARD TO KNOW HOW TO HELP THE BLACK COMMUNITY

It's what I started out to do: help people. It's hard to know where to start when many of the problems they need help with are actually caused by the police.

People everywhere need help every day. Police have training to help with many of those problems, and community policing helps the police learn more about the problems the community needs help with. But over-policing does the opposite, creating a divide between police and the people we serve. It causes fewer people to call us for help when they need it. I work for a police department that is failing at helping the people we serve.

If you are not Black or brown or poor, you don't see this reality in your own life. Most people have very little interaction with police if they live in a middle-class white neighborhood. Three traffic stops a year would be a lot! Maybe saying hi to a smiling special duty officer at a local festival is all the interaction they get if they're a good driver.

In Columbus, there are young Black men in the Black neighborhoods east of downtown who complain of being constantly stopped by police. These are called consensual stops, because the officer asks for permission to look at their ID or search their car, but often the citizen is too afraid to say no even though it is within his rights. If the citizen says no, the officer should walk away. But the citizen usually agrees to the search, feeling that the officer will search them anyway or it might look as if they had something to hide. I always tell people that if an officer asks you to do something, it's because they have to. An officer wouldn't ask for permission if he had the legal authority to search you or take your ID without it.

They don't even have to be driving to be stopped. Just walking down the street is cause for them to be stopped, patted down, and asked for their ID. Walking or driving while Black is very real. The same thing that I witnessed while on patrol with my training officer in 1997 is still happening in 2020 in the same area of town.

In 2015 there was a precinct-wide attack on citizens in this area. Eventually a citizen came into IAB and complained of being racially profiled by an officer. When the IAB investigator looked for the cruiser video to review, he discovered multiple traffic stops by many officers in that precinct. They would stop the vehicle, search it, and let the driver leave if they did not find any firearms in the car. If the officer found marijuana, he would stomp it into the ground instead of taking it to the property room. If the citizen had a warrant for their arrest, the officer wouldn't arrest them. The officer had one objective—to find guns, regardless of the rules. The investigator determined that the entire precinct was engaging in this conduct. But Chief Jacobs limited the investigation to one day of videos and told the investigator to leave the rest of the evidence he discovered out of his investigation.

During a special program during the summer, additional plainclothes officers would patrol the area. I can't stress enough how these kinds of actions rumble like earthquakes through the Black community well beyond the inner city. Many citizens have lost all trust in the police. It is similar to what we might call "occupied territories" when we see a military guard control checkpoints and public movement of citizens of a neighboring country.

This strategy of over-policing continues in Columbus even without the quotas that other police departments may still have. The daily activity of our patrol officers is not measured by stops or arrests or weapons seized or other quantifiable outcomes. We have no specific target number for people arrested, yet people might still believe we do given our behavior.

Calls for service have dropped to an all-time low in Zone 5—not because they don't have problems we could help with, but because when they call for help they are harassed. In Zone 2, farther out east, we would have twenty to thirty calls waiting for an officer to arrive compared to the predominantly Black neighborhoods on the near east side or a little to the north in Linden, where two or three were regularly waiting on any given day. There are only so many people who live in any given neighborhood. It doesn't take long before everyone knows someone who has been harassed, and they stop trusting the police.

The communities have had to become more self-sufficient in many ways. In other ways, this lack of legitimate, positive support from the government leaves a vacuum where gangs can develop more power. This in turn emboldens the police to be even more aggressive, and the over-policing escalates in an upward spiral of violence.

There is a debate about "bad apples" in police departments. Some people think that if we just get rid of those few "bad apples," all will be fine. In a wealthy part of town, the "bad apples" who acted badly in a Black neighborhood might be as sweet as apple pie. The officers who are considered overly aggressive because they use excessive force on citizens in low-income, predominantly Black neighborhoods can be assigned to a predominantly white middle-class neighborhood where they will treat the citizens less aggressively and with more respect. The exact same officers.

We are taught to treat different people differently. There are officers who believe people in some neighborhoods just need to be cursed at because they wouldn't understand respectful language. But more importantly, the thinking goes that rich white people are not the enemy—Black and brown and poor white people are.

I'm worried about the next person of color who will be brutalized without justification—true justification, not police justification. We do have power and protections that regular citizens don't have, but these rights are derived from the Constitution. The police department cheats the Constitution daily, and no one is holding us accountable. In fact, the opposite is happening. We are just getting better at defending violent officers from facing the justice system.

The Columbus Division of Police is creating the illusion that we are finding ways to communicate with the community. It's all just talk—propaganda. They are not interacting with the Black community in a positive way at all. They do photo shoots for Facebook and Twitter, but that doesn't reflect the reality. There are no boots on the ground trying to create true relationships—the police are much too busy sending our youth into the prison pipeline.

Building relationships between the Columbus Division of Police and the Black community starts at the top with the chief, who sets the tone for the entire division. When Chief Thomas Quinlan took over as interim chief in 2019 he had an opportunity to reassign officers to neighborhoods where calls for service were the highest. He didn't do it. If he had reallocated the division personnel, that would have been a great start to show that he understands the dynamics of each community and their needs.

Implementing a community policing philosophy in all aspects of our police department would go a long way toward building relationships with the residents. There are residents around the city who can truly use our help to be safe, but we are not offering them safety right now. Instead we are creating hardship and heartache. At the same time, there are residents in busy areas in the far southeast side of town who have to wait for an officer to respond to their call because of understaffing. We are putting them in danger too.

Real policing is taking reports and offering community service. Many young officers, especially, see real policing as getting guns and drugs off the streets—that's the exciting work that gives them an adrenaline rush. Valuable relationships with the community are being destroyed or not even started because these young officers are not taught the value of community policing—and how solving crimes can be done by building relationships of trust.

It's important that we train them that every piece of policing is important and they all go hand in hand. The calls for defunding the police have some validity because officers are overloaded with tasks that should be handled by social service agencies. Distributing Narcan to overdose victims, responding on calls with defibrillators, and dealing with people that are experiencing mental health issues are all things that can be handled by someone else. This is not community policing, and it's not policing.

The community leaders are well aware of the decades of systemic racism that have led to the difficult conditions in our historically segregated neighborhoods. They also know that we won't be able to police our way out of this, especially when the police continue to uphold and defend the same culture of racism that caused the problems to begin with. But any public policy shifts that try to deal systemically with the problems run into a brick wall when it gets to the division and the union that represents its officers.

As the second-shift lieutenant for patrol in Zone 2 from June of 2014 to March of 2020, I supervised the busiest shift in the division, covering a large, racially diverse area on the far east and south side of town. I didn't have trouble keeping officers focused on calls to help citizens. We had little time for anything else. In fact, I had to carve out time for them to do what we call self-initiated activity. This is where officers would look for suspicious activity, make traffic stops, or stop citizens that they believe might be participating in criminal activity. It's healthy for officers to occasionally make their presence known in the community. They can pick up on suspicious activity and deter crime.

While I was in that position I knew a lot of things that might have happened did not, simply because I was there. I could make sure that Black people and poor people were treated fairly. When I saw problems in the behavior of the officers, I called it out and tried to correct it. When I would review investigations, I would ensure that I was objective and would not immediately side with the officer. I would read the entire investigation, and I would formulate my recommendation based on the evidence. Sometimes I would decide for the citizen, and other times I would decide for the officer. The system has a tendency to automatically lean in favor of the officer. Many people don't know their rights or have enough money to hire an attorney, and the division takes advantage of that.

One thing that is very surprising to me is how this war against the Black community can recruit Black people to participate. I was riding along with a Black officer one day when he abruptly stopped the car, jumped out, and ran over to a Black man sitting in his car. Later we stopped for dinner, and I asked him what that was all about. The officer told me that he could have been a drug dealer and he wanted to harass him. I immediately responded that even if he was a drug dealer, it doesn't mean he needed to be harassed. Even bad people are good sometimes.

He then turned to a white couple sitting near us at the restaurant and asked, "Do you think that drug dealers need to be harassed?" They nodded in agreement. He had started to believe the nonsense that racist culture had been teaching him, until he became a victim of their racist attitudes himself when the division targeted him with harsh discipline for a minor violation.

There are not many supervisors in the Columbus Division of Police who will routinely correct their officers for bad behavior. This is very different from the military culture where anything that someone does rolls up to their superior, who will also have to answer for the conduct. This doesn't happen in the Columbus Division of Police. We never view the supervising sergeants or lieutenants as bearing any responsibility for the bad behavior of those that report to them. So why would they care enough to change the brutal behavior?

Not all officers in Black neighborhoods ignore service in their policing strategy, but the majority are in warrior mode, waging war on the Black community. In 1999 the US Department of Justice wanted to issue a consent decree over the Columbus Division of Police because of disproportionate use of force against African Americans. The current City of Columbus website brags that they are one of the few police departments in the country that "beat" this decree from the feds. Twenty years later, the Matrix report, commissioned by the City of Columbus, proved through extensive research that nothing has changed. We have data independently generated that proves Columbus police officers continue to disproportionately use force against African Americans. We have academic research that shows over-policing doesn't deter crime. But all of this means nothing to an officer who thinks their job is to go to war with Black people.

The Report on the Police Division Operational Review, Columbus, Ohio, prepared by the Matrix Consulting Group and released on August 19, 2019, is 330 pages of data and analysis of conditions that many people already knew, but had no data to support their currently lived experiences.

Matrix conducted a community survey to determine attitudes toward the Columbus Division of Police. Of the 35 percent who had personal contact with a division officer in the last year, only 43 percent of those responding said all officers show respect, with white people reporting 30 percent more respect than Black people. The police got a 74 percent overall favorable rating, compared to trash collectors at 82 percent and firefighters at 94 percent. Only 60 percent of respondents gave the division an excellent rating.

White and Black officers who responded to the survey reported very different experiences regarding discrimination and bias in the police department. Overall, 29 percent of the officers reported having witnessed discrimination, but 70 percent of the Black officers had, while only 25 percent of the white officers reported seeing it. Nearly 30 percent of the Black officers reported seeing bias against a member of the public in the last five years. Only 8 percent of the white officers had seen the same bias.

The report also revealed a significant disparity in the use of force against citizens of color and strongly recommended that the division increase training on de-escalation and procedural justice among other important strategies that could increase accountability, transparency, and safety.

For many years most Black officers hired by Columbus were assigned to the Black neighborhoods in Columbus, at first on foot patrol, and then in cruisers without radios. As we began to achieve equal opportunity protections, we were able to work in other neighborhoods and in other units. I personally can see the relief on a Black person's face when they see me—a Black officer—get out of my cruiser. Having even one Black officer at a scene can change the dynamic and save a life. But this is not an endorsement for sending only Black officers on calls in Black neighborhoods. We should not be solely relying on our young Black patrol officers to continue to try to reform this racist environment from the bottom up.

However we change the system of policing here and in other communities, there are some core issues that I feel would be helpful: 1) Reduce the number of police officers overall and assign them appropriately by calls for service; 2) Increase the officer training on basic issues of racism and poverty so they develop empathy and can understand how they fit into the solutions to those problems; 3) Eliminate all race-based teaching that allows these counterproductive strategies to continue to exist. In other words, stop the war on Black people. It helps no one and hurts everyone.

Before this can happen, the mayor, the safety director, the police chief, and the president of the FOP all have to examine what is in their hearts. They need to develop a genuine connection with the Black community and establish trust.

The community needs to see that they are sincere and not just ambushing them again. The rank and file need to understand that they will be rewarded for upholding the new culture of service. Safety is knowing that our police officers have a good relationship with everyone in the community and are ready to help them when they call. Columbus, Ohio, does not have that right now.

8

POLICE BRUTALITY
IS STILL OK

After decades of brutality, the advent of cell phones and dashcam videos finally let the public see what was happening. But the Columbus Division of Police and the Fraternal Order of Police are sure the public is wrong about this one.

A Black recruit in 1976 described a warning he received at the Columbus Police Academy in an interview for *The Lantern*, The Ohio State University newspaper. He said they were told not to take on a "John Wayne" or "John Shaft" attitude and not to think of themselves as "supercops" trying to take on the world single-handedly or to bully people they deal with. His trainer explained that, "Since an officer deals with the lowest element, morally, if his objectivity leaves he becomes sarcastic toward society as a whole. If that happens, his work changes for the worse."

Forty-five years later, we have moved way past sarcastic and bullying to combative and brutalizing. The public was not used to seeing these violent interactions between police and the public, except in scripted scenes on television where the bad guy was cast as evil enough to appear to deserve whatever injuries he received, until YouTube and Facebook changed all that.

The cell phone video and body cam footage now seen by the public are of interactions where most likely the person had not threatened the officer enough to justify the level of force used. These videos go viral and, understandably, enrage the general public who are then motivated to call for changes in policing.

Then two things routinely and predictably happen. First, the police make vague, noncommittal public statements. We will issue pronouncements like "This doesn't align with our values," "Everything will be done to bring justice in this case," and "The investigation is ongoing." Every so often a statement will imply officers have feelings: "Our hearts go out to the family." But more often, the statements show support for the bravery and duty of the officers involved, especially when the union leaders chime in.

Often the mayor and city council will also chime in. They will be receiving messages of disapproval from the public and might express their collective opinions behind the scenes to the safety director, who is appointed by the mayor.

Second, we wait for the public uproar to die down. The disciplinary system runs its course, which means that little, if any, discipline is handed out. In the very rare case where the safety director we report to dares to fire an officer, the union goes to work to restore the officer's job.

The officers exposed in these videos work in the Patrol Bureau or in special units that interact with the public, like Special Weapons and Tactics (SWAT) and the Narcotics Unit. Each officer has a chain of command that includes their sergeant, lieutenant, commander, deputy chief, and then the chief. Above the chief, in Columbus the city safety director, a political appointee of the mayor, has supervisory power, and he or she reports to the mayor, who is elected directly by voters.

When there is a use of force by an officer, the chain of command reviews that officer's action to determine whether the incident was within the bounds of policy. But it doesn't matter what our official policy dictates because the chain of command often thinks the brutality toward citizens is not only justified but necessary. As bad as it looks on the cell phone video and body-worn camera footage that gets out, it is actually worse. The general public has no idea how many brutal officers we have.

If a case isn't picked up by the media, the videos might never be seen by anyone who may consider the brutality to be inappropriate or worse. I have seen cases where I knew that the supervisor was covering for the officer, but I couldn't prove it.

In one case, an officer was looking for a shoplifter and asked a homeowner if he could come onto his property. The homeowner said no, so the officer reached over the fence and slapped him. The incident was caught on the homeowner's security camera. This is assault—there was no possible scenario where this would be appropriate behavior for anyone, especially a trained officer. This officer's punishment was a thirty-two hour suspension with leave forfeiture. That means thirty-two hours were deducted from his vacation leave bank, which is where our vacation hours accumulate each pay period until we want to use the hours to take time off with pay. The public hears that the officer was punished with a suspension, but the officer goes back to work the next day with no loss in pay.

This violent behavior makes me wonder if the division attracts recruits who are predisposed to violence, or if the officers learn to behave violently after they go through our training and assimilate into our culture. Either way, most supervisors are not working to shut down the excessive use of force. This points to another key distinction between supervisory duties in policing versus the military units where I served. In the Columbus Division of Police, as a supervisor, my performance is not rated by the performance of my unit. Because of the union contract, my pay rate is guaranteed based on my rank. My rank is only determined by my ability to pass the next test. If an officer working under me is disciplined for using excessive force, that would never show up in my work record as that officer's supervisor, or prevent me from moving up in rank.

Another video captured an officer slamming a woman to the ground onto her face for no justified reason. This was a brutal attack causing her pain and injury. I found him out of policy, and he resigned before his discipline was determined by the chief.

The law gives officers the authority to use reasonable force, up to and including deadly force. We are trained to know the minimum amount of force necessary, and we are given weapons to use so that we have choices. We are taught techniques that inflict the least amount of pain and injury to complete the arrest while keeping ourselves safe.

The privilege we have to use force to defend ourselves and complete an arrest is being exploited by some officers who enjoy mistreating disenfranchised people. They are not just targeting Black residents anymore—poor whites, the homeless, LGBTQ people, immigrants, the mentally ill, and most recently Black Lives Matter protestors are all at risk for mistreatment. The racist mentality has emboldened some officers to brutalize everyone who they see as "other." They show no remorse for their actions. They punish people they feel have disrespected them, but they rationalize that these human beings deserve no respect themselves because they are "less than."

After a struggle in a convenience store with a suspect in September of 2017, Officer Joseph Bogard was taped saying he wanted to choke the life out of Timothy Davis. The case became a top story in the local media and was picked up by national media.

Immediately, while the media was watching, Chief Jacobs expressed disapproval, took away Bogard's badge and gun, and put him on desk duty while IAB investigated. Mayor Ginther applauded the chief for her swift action. The FOP president nonchalantly said it all looked okay to him. After the investigation, Bogard was given a written reprimand and restored to his previous duty.

The division rarely finds a use of force on a citizen outside of policy, but when they do, the discipline is light. Officers who take too much time off work when they don't have enough time banked get harsher punishment than an officer who threatens to choke a suspect on camera. Supervisors have handed out more discipline for losing an ID badge than for kicking a suspect twice in the butt after he was handcuffed and on the ground.

I don't think this has changed much in twenty years. Before I was a sergeant I didn't pay much attention to how discipline really worked. Now I know that use-of-force violations are rarely disciplined with suspensions. In the rare cases when they are, the officer can be given a leave forfeiture option, like the officer who slapped the homeowner over his fence. Not exactly a harsh punishment.

Leave forfeiture is basically almost being suspended. When an officer is suspended with this option, they sign the following "Acceptance of Leave Forfeiture Option" agreement:

> I agree to forfeit _____ hours of accrued leave as follows:
> _____ vacation hours
> _____ overtime hours
> _____ holiday hours
>
> In doing so, I realize that I will not be required to serve a suspension from duty. This shall constitute a final disposition of the matter.

In a sampling of cases over the last few years, I found that officers have forfeited a range of hours for a variety of violations:

- 40 hours for two counts of unlawful restraint
- 80 hours for operating a vehicle under the influence
- 120 hours for having sex with a prostitute while off duty
- 32 hours for offering to pay for sex
- 16 hours for failing to conduct an investigation
- 16 hours for throwing flares at vehicles while working traffic
- 16 hours for calling in a complaint on the chief of police
- 96 hours for kicking a suspect in the head while unconscious
- 8 hours for striking a driver with a car door
- 16 hours for placing a foot on an intoxicated suspect's neck

Use-of-force violations often receive only write ups (DCCs). Examples I found include incidents of macing, striking with a flashlight, and kicking in the face or butt.

Out of thirty-nine disciplinary cases I examined from 2015 through the beginning of 2020, 70 percent were given the leave forfeiture or a write-up. Out of the remaining 30 percent, nine were given a suspension and three were terminated.

A very public case shows how far the union is willing to go to preserve our ability to brutalize citizens. Officer Zachary Rosen was already known to the Black community in Columbus after he was not disciplined or indicted for the use of deadly force against Henry Green in 2016. The following year he was captured on cell phone video stomping on the head of a suspect lying handcuffed on his stomach.

His use of force was reviewed by his chain of command. Everyone ruled that stomping the citizen in the head was within policy, except for the deputy chief, who ruled that the stomp to the head was outside of policy. Chief Jacobs recommended a three-day suspension, which was surprising. And then, even more surprising, when the action reached the safety director for review, Rosen was fired. For a minute, it felt like we had a city government that was tired of the brutality and was willing to tell the police to work within our rules and our training.

As normal, the criminal justice system deferred to the internal discipline system within the police department, so Rosen was not charged with assault. With qualified immunity—a legal provision that shields certain public servants from civil actions—it meant that the victim could not sue Rosen personally for damages. The victim did, however, receive a settlement from the city.

Then the union rose to his defense. They held fundraisers for Officer Rosen, bought billboards, and represented him throughout his grievance process. A year later, an arbitrator awarded him his job back. Community activists were livid and waged their own public relations campaign, buying billboards emblazoned with Rosen's picture to warn area residents to watch out for him. Fearing for his safety, Chief Jacobs took him off the street and reassigned him to a coveted assignment in a detective unit, a job officers usually must wait many years to get.

There is one exception to the justice system steering clear of officer behavior. When an officer causes a death, the county prosecutor takes the case to the grand jury to determine if the deadly force was within the acceptable actions to do our job and protect ourselves. In all the uses of deadly force in the Columbus Division of Police since I have been here, only one officer has been indicted for murder. He is a Black officer who killed a white woman.

One officer who wasn't indicted for using deadly force was Brian Mason. He had used deadly force against four other people, two of whom were fatal, in the nine years he had been with the division when he shot and killed thirteen-year-old Tyre King. I was at lunch on September 14, 2016, with a lieutenant from the zone where Tyre was killed when the call went out for an "officer-involved shooting." We responded to the scene.

I was devastated when I saw how little the victim's body was. He was lying on the ground in handcuffs, his toy gun lying several feet away. As the paramedics put him in the ambulance, I saw Tyre's face and realized he was just a child.

As a mother and a police officer, I've had a hard time with this. I couldn't imagine how he would have pointed a fake gun at an officer, as the report says he did. He knew it was a fake. He might have been trying to throw it away. He couldn't have been using it to try to defend himself—he was old enough to know it might get him killed. He had likely heard of Tamir Rice, a twelve-year-old Cleveland boy who had been killed two years earlier playing in a park with a toy gun. It has never made sense to me.

Tyre's death continues to bring pain to his family and our community. But the division and the FOP do not share that pain. As police we are wired to defend our actions and blame the victims for their deaths. This is the hardest part of the thin black line: feeling the pain of the community I am a part of and knowing that the system I work for denies the pain even exists.

Most officers go their entire careers without shooting at anyone. When I looked up the statistics on excessive use of force in the Columbus Division of Police, out of 1,900 officers, I learned that fewer than one hundred officers account for half of the cases in the division. I'm concerned about all the officers still on the job with years of incidents involving excessive use of force. Normally as an officer ages, our priorities change. If we started out in the warrior mentality, out to get the "bad guy," we usually mellow as we settle into our careers. But these one hundred officers don't seem to be mellowing. And many of the other 1,800 officers continue to cover for them.

From my social work education I learned to connect this behavior with post-traumatic stress disorder (PTSD), a mental condition often associated with military combat. As policing becomes increasingly militarized, and our mindset changes into a warrior force, we see more PTSD in police officers.

Once an officer experiences a trauma like a use of deadly force, their brain changes. These changes make them more reactive to the next situation where they might feel danger. Think of someone jumping when they hear a loud noise. That is normal, but a person with PTSD might also feel tremendous danger from hearing that noise, with no imminent threat. So when an officer reports that they felt threatened by a suspect, it might not be the current situation causing that reaction.

Unlike the real military, police don't connect the dots. We don't anticipate this mental health issue in our officers, and we send them right back out to inflict more trauma on the community, and themselves. Instead we should be training officers not to create the trauma in the first place. But as police officers, we also experience trauma that we don't create. It is my wish for that trauma to be healed and not lead to more tragic deaths.

9

THE DEVIL IS IN THE CONTRACT DETAILS

The Fraternal Order of Police has a 174-page union contract with the City of Columbus that appears to protect every sworn employee equally. So why doesn't it work that way?

Even though the Fraternal Order of Police's national constitution states that "Race, creed, or color shall be no bar," their actions over the years have created a nationwide cultural divide and prompted anti-racist groups to hold demonstrations at their national events.

The elected leadership of the local chapter are officers from the Columbus Division of Police. Some continue to work their regular assignments and others are on release time, paid by donations of vacation time from FOP members. About half of the members are from the division; the rest are from twenty-eight other law enforcement agencies in Franklin County. The voting base that elects the leadership is predominantly male and white. The culture from the division spills over into their work at the union—they have shown no interest in eliminating the racist culture at the division.

The FOP is important in allowing the culture of discrimination within the division to continue unabated. The rules in the contract are clearly unbiased on paper. But as minority officers, when our supervisors break the rules and we try to defend ourselves, we have to ask for the union's help, and the help they offer does not come without bias. The union also allows the high-ranking officers to bend and break a lot of rules in backroom deals in exchange for other favors. These favors rarely flow in the direction of Black and women officers.

The union does offer legal representation to its members for on-duty serious investigations of misconduct. However, going to arbitration is strictly a call that is made by the president of the union. This is a process that brings in a third-party arbitrator to decide a dispute between an officer and their employer, the city. It is a right we have that can prevent the cost and hassle of a lawsuit to demand fair and legal treatment.

There doesn't appear to be any rationale for which cases are sent to arbitration. The union took the case of one white male officer, accused of hiring prostitutes while on duty, to arbitration. At the same time, they would not go to arbitration for a Black male officer fired for an accusation of untruthfulness. Two cases of white officers accused of untruthfulness at the same time resulted in one having the charges converted to unbecoming conduct. The other had his charges sustained but received a 240 hour suspension and was placed on the liar list. Neither was fired. No one is publishing statistics on this of course, but it seems difficult for Black officers to receive the same considerations when we need it the most.

The union officials see the trends of disparity in discipline based on race and gender but choose not to do anything about it. This impacts Black officers because our conduct violations are disciplined more severely compared to those of white officers. It also affects citizens who are the victims of police brutality when the officer's use-of-force violations are ignored, or worse, defended as necessary, while lesser offenses become big news stories.

Officers often work overtime and special duty shifts. We also earn vacation time for days off based on how long we have been on the job. A Black officer, Kevin Morgan, was accused of receiving pay for nine shifts that he didn't work. The union did not negotiate a settlement agreement. He maintained that he had worked the shifts on a flexible schedule and the special duty assignment coordinator had made an error. The city prosecutor reviewed the case and declined to press charges for theft in office. The internal investigation, however, sustained the allegations. Morgan was fired. He then sued for damages in federal court, and his case is still pending.

In contrast to Morgan's case, in 2014 white male sergeants Bronson Constable and Doug Jones stole thousands of dollars from the division by getting paid for work they did not perform. They were caught and ordered to pay back the money. The union represented them by reaching a settlement agreement. They each got a six-week unpaid suspension as discipline. The city prosecutor declined to press charges.

The FOP has the ability to amplify this disparity by holding fundraisers, buying billboards, and using other public relations tactics for white officers who they choose to support. They once told me that they would not take one of my cases to arbitration because "people don't like you." There is no appeal for this type of discrimination other than to handle our own cases without the help of the union.

The union contract section 5.1 is a joint pledge that states:

> The City and the Lodge shall not discriminate against any member on the basis of the member's age, race, color, sex, creed, religion, ancestry, marital status, veteran's status, military status, political affiliation, national origin, disability, or sexual orientation as provided by law.

Despite this very clear wording, minority and female officers cannot file a grievance stating that this section of the contract has been violated. When we file our complaints with IAB, the person we accuse of discrimination (the focus) is then represented by the union in their investigation.

The person filing the complaint can receive some union services, including a grievance representative. Over the past 24 years, I have filed multiple EEO complaints, an unfair labor practice against the union, and lawsuits in order to fight back against the oppressive system designed to make me fail. All of this combined has cost my husband and me well over $100,000 in legal fees. I have also helped others file several complaints against the division.

Equal employment opportunity cases are the biggest challenge we have as employees who face discrimination based on race and gender. When the City of Columbus refuses to address the issues we raise—as they usually do—we have the option to take our case to the Ohio Civil Rights Commission (OCRC), the state agency that hears cases of discrimination for employees in Ohio. To have the best chance of winning our case we need to hire a lawyer and then wait for up to a year for them to investigate and issue a decision. During that time we must continue to work in an often even more hostile environment.

On other complaints against supervisors that are not EEO–related claims, police officers filing complaints can also face challenges with our union representation. The union seems to protect certain supervisors by putting little or no effort into our representation, especially if they are friends with the focus, who is the supervisor or officer the complaint is filed against.

We know which officers are closely connected to division management. We know who will be protected if an investigation opens up on them. On the flip side, we know that if someone who is not connected gets in trouble, they will not receive the same effort. Those of us who are not favored feel very hurt by this—when we aren't treated the same, it makes us discouraged and angry. We see other officers getting opportunities they haven't earned, and we wonder if there is anything we could ever do just to be treated fairly.

These discriminatory attitudes of union leaders and division management are apparent in their treatment of Black police officers in the discipline and grievance systems, their treatment of Black citizens as they file complaints against officers, and their determination of appropriate use of force against Black people. Thinking of all the ways racism is alive and well within the division can make your head spin—it seems like it's a reflex, something that feels so normal to them that they can't see it for what it is.

Born out of the slave patrols of the early eighteenth century, policing continues to carry out the foundational principle that Black people are the enemy and the police are here to conquer them. There is overt collusion among officers to maintain this offensive. At a recent George Floyd protest in front of the Ohio Statehouse, there was a call and response between the protesters shouting, "Black lives matter!" and the officers presumably there to protect them yelling back, "Blue lives matter!"

It's common to see answers to questions at an IAB interview where one officer states, "I don't recall," to each question asked about another officer. I have often wondered why we hire officers with such bad memories. I also know that they clearly remember times I corrected their behavior by asking them to follow the rules or disagreed with how they reported a brutal incident. They even remembered that night at roll call when I called out illegal vehicle searches, twenty-two years later!

The police department does a very good job of keeping systems of discrimination hidden from the public and even its own employees. People can't pick out the patterns of corruption unless they get a top-down view like the safety director or chief has. Everything is compartmentalized into bureaus—an officer working in one bureau, such as Patrol, has no idea what is happening in the Detective Bureau or Traffic Bureau down the hall. If we are on the ground level, we are very limited in what we know because our only source of information is the rumor mill. We are spread out across 223 square miles in several substations made up of multiple bureaus, working three shifts, seven days a week. We don't all even hear the same rumors.

I didn't understand how the discrimination I faced fit into a bigger picture for quite a while. From my interview process at the police academy to the retaliation during my field training to my treatment in the Training Bureau, I didn't know that I wasn't the only one that this stuff was happening to. As I became a sergeant in 2009 after fourteen years on the job, I saw how my attitudes about discipline, use of force, and other key issues differed from my chain of command. I started to understand.

As a lieutenant since 2014, I have seen even more of the racist strategies at work inside the police department with personnel and outside the department with the public. When I started to realize that the way we bend and break our own rules is the same thing we do when dealing with the public at large, I started to see the patterns more clearly— the two are so intertwined they can't really be split apart and dealt with separately. It is all the same war against Black people.

One of the most difficult things to prove in policing is racial profiling. Black people know when we are pulled over for no reason other than our skin color. We know when we are harassed or hurt, and we have the right to request an investigation into that officer's behavior. When I was investigating these complaints as a sergeant in the IAB, I saw the patterns of the officers who were the frequent offenders. These complaints are rarely, if ever, sustained and disciplined.

When Chief Jacobs took office in 2012, she eliminated the deputy chief position over Internal Affairs, giving her more direct supervisory power over citizen complaints. This change in the chain of command gave her more control of the outcomes of the investigations before they were sent back to the supervisor for discipline. Who would benefit the most from a decrease in citizen complaints or a decrease in sustained allegations? Her record as chief appears to be an eight-year period with almost no racial profiling and fewer citizen complaints.

One simple way the police can discriminate both internally and externally is in how we conduct investigations. The citizen filing an Internal Affairs complaint against an officer will be interviewed first. The contract allows the officer to listen to the citizen's interview and review all the evidence prior to being interviewed by the IAB investigator. If the investigator is biased against a Black or female officer, and doesn't want them to have an advantage, or just doesn't like the officer, they will interview them at the beginning of the investigation instead of the end.

If the investigator interviews the officer first, the officer only has access to a small amount of evidence to review prior to the interview. This eliminates the advantage the officer usually has of having access to all the evidence prior to the interview. Normally the investigator will interview them last so they have their best chance of getting cleared of misconduct.

This gives the officer access to their body-worn camera footage and other evidence collected by the investigator. They can usually wait a few days to collect their thoughts, get a union rep, and determine their strategy for the interview. This all benefits the officer. If the investigator changes any of these rules, even subtly, the officer can be at a disadvantage. The order of interviews seems like a simple thing, but when applied inconsistently it can result in discriminatory outcomes.

After an investigation, the investigator recommends a finding of sustained, not sustained, or unfounded. Their decision goes up the chain of command at Internal Affairs, who all review the finding and then forward the investigation to the officer's chain of command for review and a recommendation. Unless it's considered critical misconduct and there is a request to deviate from lower level discipline, the officer's deputy chief makes the final determination. In some critical misconduct cases, the chief makes the final decision.

Discipline is very decentralized and a powerful source of control and intimidation over minority officers. Even with each sergeant having written guidance on how to pick a level of discipline, treatment of different officers can vary widely from sergeant to sergeant. In the union contract it looks like there are safeguards to make sure discipline is not discriminatory, but there is no way for each officer to know if their discipline was fair. The union leadership knows that it is not fair but does nothing to stop the unfairness.

A clear example of this happened while I was a patrol lieutenant. I had two white male officers fail to take a police report of a home burglary even though the homeowner had specifically asked them to take one. The homeowner filed a complaint, and the IAB investigation found that the officers should have taken a report. The officers' sergeant and I recommended documented constructive counseling (DCC), which is the lowest level of discipline and remains in their file for nine months. A written reprimand would stay for three years. Our commander, Rhonda Grizzell, said that Chief Quinlan, who was new at the time, was encouraging more positive corrective action (PCA), which is not considered discipline and is not placed in our file. So my recommendation was overridden by Grizzell, and the officers received PCA, essentially no discipline at all.

During the same time period, the third-shift lieutenant in the same zone had two Black officers fail to take a report when they responded to a call of a woman damaging the homeowner's property. Even though the homeowner did not specifically ask for a report, an IAB investigation determined that one should have been taken. The officers' sergeant and the lieutenant recommended a DCC as well, and Grizzell agreed. Same conduct. Different discipline.

I went to one of the Black officers and told her she needed to file a grievance on her discipline. She had no way to know that the chief's encouragement to use more positive corrective action did not apply to her as a Black female officer. I filed a third-party complaint that our commander discriminated when applying discipline. The officer got her DCC thrown out through the grievance process at the safety director's office, but the IAB investigator found that the commander did not discriminate. I was not surprised.

We have a disciplinary tracking system that we are supposed to use for determining the most appropriate level of discipline. We can look up a specific rule of conduct and see which discipline was handed out for that violation in the past, not unlike a judge consulting with past cases to see what sentence a defendant deserves. When we document our choice of discipline we cite the previous conduct violations. On paper that sounds fair, but a supervisor can pick and choose the previous cases that match their preference for the severity of the discipline.

I recently learned that a lieutenant, who still had access to an older database from a previous assignment, was going back to 2008 to find harsher discipline examples to use as comparisons. It often feels as minority officers, that discipline is handed out randomly, with so many ways around the rules.

Another problem we have with our discipline system is that the sergeants have some leeway in how they pick the code of conduct violation. It's like when a protester is standing in the street during a demonstration—they could be given a ticket for jaywalking, a misdemeanor with a fine. Or they could be arrested for obstructing traffic, a much more serious charge. We can do a similar thing when picking a code of conduct violation if we want to give someone a harsher level of discipline.

I am not advocating for anything other than having rules help us do our job to protect our community and then having those rules followed equitably. When I discipline an officer, I know it fixes the behavior when I'm in the room. But I also know when I look the other way, it's business as usual. A white officer told me the other day that he used to be afraid of me because I am a no-nonsense lieutenant. Then he rode with a friend of mine and learned more about how I think about things. He said he now understands that I just want the rules applied fairly to everyone.

I had a lot of experience dealing with rank and discipline levels in the military. We earned our rank, and everyone at that rank was treated the same and had to follow the same rules. This was one of the biggest shocks to my system moving over to nonmilitary policing—when they handed out tasks and discipline, it seemed to matter to everyone what gender or race an officer was. I've seen many minority officers receive harsher discipline that others with the same violation were not subjected to.

The tactics used to get around the unbiased contractual practices are nothing new. They are cleverly adjusted as technology or politicians catch us using them. When Chief Jackson was a lieutenant in the early 1970s, he started the first minority recruiting unit. As chief in the 2000s, his executive staff newsletter continuously reported that minority and women officers were being disciplined at a higher rate. Even as a Black chief, he did not have the power to make systemic changes that might have prevented the discrimination that persists today.

The union even allows themselves to be a tool for division retaliation. In 2018, Frank Miller, an officer I had never met, sent a letter to the union asking for my removal due to an ethics violation. He had submitted the letter with the help of Commander Jennifer Knight. I knew this because it was an exact copy of a previous letter she had written about someone else, with the name changed but not the pronouns! This was another attempt by Knight to retaliate against me for standing up against discrimination.

A Facebook post calling for everyone to show up to vote for my removal was at first vague about who they were talking about.

Dean Worthington is a white convicted felon who served ninety days in jail for pandering sexually oriented material involving a minor. Before he resigned from the Columbus Division of Police, he was our public information officer. But Miller, a person who has never met me, would rather throw me out? The union's ethics committee conducted an investigation, determined that I did not violate their ethics rules, and dismissed the case. Smells of retaliation to me!

🔒 facebook.com

8 hrs   Like   Reply   More

Ken Bowers

Because I really don't care who I offend are we talking about McFadden or Worthington. Just a simple yes or no will suffice.

👍 1

8 hrs   Like   Reply   More

Frank Miller

The first one

Ken Bowers

Thank you

8 hrs   Like   Reply   More

Frank Miller

So we are looking for the FOP to remove Lt. McFadden as a member of our union! We need to show up and show that there is overwhelming support for this move. Because there will be fallout from it! So if you agree I am asking you to show up and support this move!!

👍💬 2

— 10 —

WHITE COP, BLACK COP, WHY IS THERE STILL A DIFFERENCE?

We had a Black police chief in Columbus for nineteen years, beginning in 1990, with a Black mayor in office for much of that time. One would think that with that brass and political muscle, they could have figured it out. But even they failed.

The racist culture within the Columbus Division of Police manifests in so many little ways for Black officers that it would be impossible to name them all. We have to pick and choose our battles to conserve energy and not get overwhelmed — we just have to ignore some things to stay sane. But we can't ignore the most terrifying thing that can happen to a Black officer: to be falsely accused of a serious crime. The threat is always there, with no known way to inoculate ourselves from the possibility of it happening to us. Here are three stories that remind us of the risk we face.

YOU FIT THE DESCRIPTION OF A RAPIST

In 2005, Robert Patton confessed to raping over fifty Columbus women over a decade in the mostly Black Linden neighborhood and the neighborhood near Ohio State's campus. He earned the nickname "Linden-area Rapist" while the crime lab was delayed in identifying him due to a backlog of DNA testing. It was definitely a big case, and we had a lot of physical descriptions of him that gave us a good idea of who we were looking for.

At the time of the rapes, the officers that patrolled the Linden area reported for work at the substation located a few blocks north near Karl and Morse Road. A Black officer named Sean Mack who lived nearby would stop in frequently to pick up a cruiser or a radio or finish some paperwork. He often picked up special duty assignments that would require him to be at the substation at different times during the night. It is not uncommon for officers to stop by substations where they are not regularly assigned. Even so, a white sergeant working there was suspicious of the random hours when Mack would show up at the substation. He thought Mack fit the description of the rape suspect we were looking for, so he reported this to his chain of command and IAB. They initiated an investigation and started following Mack in order to retrieve a sample of his DNA, which they did.

Jerome Barton, a Black sergeant, found out about the investigation and got upset about it. Barton knew Mack had been with the division for ten years and had no reason to be suspected. He didn't even fit the description of the suspect—except that he was Black. Barton was the first person to tell Mack that he was being investigated for these crimes.

YOU FIT THE DESCRIPTION OF A JOHN

There was a Black sergeant who worked in IAB when I worked there. Two white officers assigned to the Vice Unit reported that they saw a prostitute get into an unmarked division vehicle driven by a man they thought looked like the IAB sergeant. They had worked with him in another unit before he became a sergeant. They filed a complaint, and an IAB investigation was started without his knowledge. Two other IAB investigators began following him around to try to catch him picking up a prostitute so that they could charge him criminally. I happened to be riding with him a couple of times to interviews but had no idea we were being followed.

They eventually located the woman and asked her who was with her that day. She told them he was an old friend who works as a bus driver. Guess who looked nothing like the sergeant?

The sergeant was very upset that he would be accused of a crime and asked the chief to remove his name from the investigation file—he did not want his name to be associated with a crime in any way and attached to an investigation for the rest of his career.

YOU FIT THE DESCRIPTION OF A THIEF

A Black officer was working on a sixty-day temp assignment in the Narcotics Bureau, which is very unusual. Following standard procedures, he logged in some cash and drugs from an arrest to the property room. Another officer reported that they couldn't locate the money in the property room so they believed this Black officer never submitted the money as required. Instead of asking the officer about the money, they automatically assumed that he stole it.

The investigators got a search warrant and came to search his home. He was there and insisted that he had turned in the cash. They called the property room clerk on duty that night and learned that it had been mislabeled in the property room — but only after they searched his body and a portion of his house.

Searching a home is a very invasive and degrading procedure. It is extremely humiliating. Imagine having your coworkers show up at your home unannounced and invade your personal space, especially when there is nothing you can do about it. Cash can be hidden almost anywhere, so the officers search every pocket of your clothing, every container of food, and every child's toy while your family is patted down and seated in a cruiser to wait for the humiliation to be over. Then it's your job to clean up your clothing and belongings strewn all over the floor and replace the breakfast cereal they dumped out.

After these types of incidents happen to an officer, it changes them. All three of these officers are scarred from their experiences—it took away their trust in the police department. To be falsely accused of committing crimes by other police officers and investigated without knowing is one of the most demoralizing things that can happen to an officer.

Consistent with systemic racism, these types of false accusations only happen with white officers accusing Black officers. We have certainly investigated white officers for criminal activity, but only to my knowledge based on citizen complaints. I haven't seen any investigations, especially during my time at IAB, where a white officer accused another white officer of a crime.

Other concerns that arise from this are two basic issues present in racism. The first is implicit bias that would cause someone to suspect a Black person of a crime so quickly, even when there is no evidence or prior behavior that would suggest criminal activity. The second stems from the challenge that some white people have of telling Black people apart. Remember that police officers are specifically trained to recognize and collect data on appearance so they can identify suspects. If that is their excuse, then they are admitting they are incompetent at one of the core skills required for doing their job well.

I hadn't been falsely accused of a crime, thankfully, even though I knew it was always a possibility. And then a similar accusation, although not criminal, happened this year during the worst week of my life. Of course.

During the first week of March of 2020, a cousin of mine was tragically killed by an accidental electrocution. Everyone knew Covid-19 was on its way into our lives, but we didn't know how to protect ourselves yet. Ohio's lockdown hadn't started and there were no travel restrictions in place, so I went to New York for the funeral. I went up on March 9 and came back two days later, the day the World Health Organization declared a pandemic. No one was sure what was happening yet, so when I got back I wore a mask to work to be safe.

In response to the pandemic, the division began activating the National Incident Management System (NIMS), an emergency management system developed by the Federal Emergency Management Agency (FEMA) that all police departments know and use. It is helpful for large incidents that span across jurisdictions, as it allows all the departments responding to be on the same page and speak the same language. I was very impressed with how they handled everything. We had briefings each day with specific objectives. Our work areas were intensively cleaned, and we were given instructions on how to minimize exposure to the virus. They gave us masks, hand sanitizers, and thermometers to check our temperature each day before we left for work. Everyone was given an extra day off each week to reduce our interaction with each other. They installed new procedures to minimize our contact with the public. I thought they did a great job and mobilized very quickly to respond to the state of emergency.

On Monday, March 23, I took my temperature like I usually did as I was getting ready to go to work. It was 100.4°F, which was the threshold for staying home. I called in sick and followed the instructions to go get tested. This was when tests were very hard to get, and police officers were in the first group allowed to get them. I was the first person to test positive in the division. It made the local news, but without identifying me.

I stayed home and isolated myself on one floor of my house away from my family until I got the results. This was the day that our governor issued stay-at-home orders for the state. By the time I learned I was positive, I had developed more symptoms and didn't want to get out of bed. It was six days before my fever broke.

While I was in bed feeling unbelievably awful, I was getting text messages from people I work with on the sixth floor of police headquarters. They told me they had received text messages asking if they saw me in the building after I was out sick and if so, on what day. I didn't understand what was happening.

A sergeant had filed a complaint against me with my supervisor that said that he had seen me in the building after I had symptoms. Had it been true, this would have been a violation of the emergency procedures that were in place. Why hadn't I heard this from my supervisor? Instead of contacting me directly, my supervisor began an investigation by texting a lot of other officers, some of whom I don't even work with and would have never been in direct contact with.

This investigation disclosed my identity as the employee with Covid to my coworkers, which was technically allowed during the pandemic, but at that time and feeling the way I did, it was very difficult to handle. My supervisor checked the security cameras and the ID card system. There was no trace of me having been in the building after I had symptoms, but yet he still needed to ask everyone they could think of but me. He finished the investigation without calling me, but instead telling everyone I had Covid.

When I figured out what happened, I called him to ask why he had talked to everyone but me. I told him that he should have checked the cameras on the eighth floor where the chiefs and deputy chiefs work, because if I had been interested in infecting anyone, I certainly would have headed straight there! He laughed.

Several of my relatives who attended the funeral also contracted the virus. Two ended up on ventilators, and one of my uncles passed away. It's likely but not proven that I caught it from attending the funeral since I didn't show any symptoms until ten days later. But because I wore a mask at work each day before I had symptoms, no one I work with became infected. My husband didn't get sick either.

Tragically, my mother, who lived with us, contracted the virus as well. She had not attended the funeral in New York, but she had been going to critical doctor's appointments and other public places, taking every precaution. She wasn't able to handle the infection on top of the other heart and breathing issues she had. She passed away in early April. It was very hard to be one of the first families in the county to lose a loved one to the pandemic. It still stings that someone would accuse me of knowingly exposing anyone to this deadly virus.

It's hard not to see this as more of the same pattern of white officers starting investigations on Black officers without our knowledge for something we likely wouldn't have done. Executing a search warrant for a clerical error, accusing a happily married man of soliciting prostitution, and calling a man a suspected rapist because he was working in a different area of town are so much worse than what happened to me. But in the throes of my grief for three family members, having just recovered from Covid myself and feeling very vulnerable to a new unknown enemy, this investigation felt just as bad. If we can't have compassion for our fellow officers at a time like this, how can we begin to have compassion for the people we serve?

After my symptoms cleared in March and I completed the mandatory waiting period to return to work, I took a few vacation days and bereavement days to say goodbye to my mom. That was a month I will never forget. And somehow, in my darkest hour, the division found a way to make it darker. It was so hurtful that anyone would think that I would do something as recklessly dangerous as exposing them to a virus that could kill them; then instead of simply talking to me directly, open an investigation and not tell me, but tell everyone else.

The Columbus Division of Police continued to install new precautions and protocols to deal with Covid. They even provided us temporary housing if we didn't want to potentially expose our family members. Overall they were handling this well—until the mask debate started. Even with a county-level mandate, a city mandate, and a division mandate, as of this writing, officers are having a hard time wearing masks. I sat through a training in July of 2020 with high-ranking supervisors, and I was the only one wearing a mask. Later that evening I learned that the deputy chief sitting next to me tested positive.

In the Columbus Division of Police, one in ten officers is Black. If we get assigned to a historically segregated unit, we might be the only Black officer there. At many smaller police departments, a Black officer might be the only one in the whole department. This gives us little clout to attack systemic racism. The bold officers of POER who took on the system in the 1980s were then systematically retaliated against until no one would join their group. Any further attempts to organize within the department over the years have been instantly squashed. Many who have tried have moved on to other departments or other careers.

Nationally, Black officers have formed their own associations since the 1970s, not necessarily to bargain but to support each other because of the systemic racism that permeates policing. I am a member of NOBLE, the National Organization of Black Law Enforcement Executives. NOBLE serves as a community outreach organization, inviting anyone of any race in or out of law enforcement to work with us to create a more racially just system. There are six hundred chapters in the US, but we only started a central Ohio chapter in 2019. It's a wonderful group of dedicated professionals, and we share many of the same challenges I have seen throughout my career.

We haven't had a space within the division to connect and encourage each other since POER was ostracized. I enjoy that benefit of NOBLE but would like them to be more politically active. Maybe as the current climate of unrest starts to lead to some policy changes, we will be able to lend our collective voice to the conversation. The POER experience here is still an open wound, and Black officers are reluctant to organize for fear of even more retaliation. NOBLE is a national organization, however, which gives us a new platform to bypass the approval of our management.

When Mayor Ginther conducted a nationwide search for a new chief last year, the runner-up candidate was Perry Tarrant, a member of NOBLE from Seattle. At a community event to meet the candidates, members of NOBLE from around the region showed up to support us. That feeling that someone had our backs was new to us.

I was determined to try to prevent the status quo leadership from continuing. After Quinlan passed me up for the watch commander position, it motivated me even more to openly support Tarrant. I created "Outside Chief for Change" stickers to pass out at the door to the community event. It was my first attempt at a campaign style effort to effect change in the division.

Our members are starting to get a seat at the policy table as well. We have two chiefs in central Ohio, and a member was appointed to the work group designing the mayor's citizen review board in Columbus. There are no people more qualified to help design a solution to the racist system that we work in than Black officers; we have fought oppression daily throughout our careers on both sides of the thin black line.

— 11 —

MENTORING, BECAUSE THERE IS NO ONE ELSE WHO CAN

As I got better at navigating the discriminatory environment, I saw how other officers needed more than mentoring to root out the corruption.

I never had a mentor. No one appeared in my life to show me the way, help me avoid the land mines and reach my goals. I only had God and my mom. Neither has ever let me down. But now I understood how a mentor with experience would have also been tremendously helpful.

As I started to gain that experience myself by trial and error—mostly error—I noticed that others around me were having trouble too. When I was planning to take the sergeant's exam in 2008, I noticed that minority officers weren't passing the test at the same rate as white officers. I didn't yet fully understand all the implications of that but applied the solution that I thought should work: studying harder.

I got in touch with several people who were ready to take the test, or had already tried and failed, and we formed a study group. We didn't have the answers to the tests, but some people did. As minorities we are used to working harder and not being able to cut corners. Since the test is graded on a curve, it is essentially a competition.

It was empowering to help each other, share frustrations, and really learn the information. Three of the four of us were promoted. I received the highest score on the test that round. It was the first time I knew of that a Black woman came out on top. That felt good, but it felt even better knowing that I had helped others during the process. It's wonderful when someone knows I have their best interest at heart and they can trust me.

Even though I had gotten my promotion, I knew we needed to keep minority officers rising in rank because we didn't have many working in the upper levels at the division. I also helped white officers advance—it's important that we have good people running the police department, regardless of race. During the next testing period, I put many more study groups together that consisted of both male and female, Black, white and Latino. Of the roughly twenty Black sergeants we currently have, over half are people who I helped achieve that rank. My mentees love it when I help them achieve a goal.

The connection I form with officers when I mentor them is really special to me. I have also helped officers in other police departments study for their promotional exams. I enjoy forming professional connections with other officers in the area. That is what people do in a healthy professional environment.

The last study group I organized met from 2011 to 2013, when I entered Capital University Law School and could no longer fit in study groups around my classes. I missed it. In the seven years since I stopped the groups, only five additional Black officers have been promoted to sergeant. The impact of mentoring is significant, providing motivation, support, community, and specific guidance to navigate the system.

Recruiting new Black officers is another area where I have been able to mentor people. Some people in the community who have become interested in entering the academy have contacted me for help, and I'm thrilled to help them study for the entrance exam. But it saddens me that I have to warn them not to disclose their relationship with me.

I don't want my history of trying to root out racism to taint these talented young people. They need to get their bearings before they take on the culture of discrimination. It's not outside the realm of possibility that they might be harassed or become the target of retaliation in response to my fight against discrimination. The mob mentality that lives in our culture might think it's a good idea to go after one of my friends.

I don't have much patience for sitting around and complaining about something while waiting for someone else to change things. I am much more comfortable trying to find out what I can do about something and then doing it. Mentoring is an amazing process that brings so many people into the problem-solving process and empowers them to help solve it. But sometimes I don't have the time to wait for someone to solve their own problems, so I put on my other helper hat—that of advocate.

When an officer believes that their employment rights negotiated under the union contract have been violated, they can file a complaint called a grievance. They are entitled to a union representative to walk them through the grievance process. Grievance reps take a course to learn how to do this. These meetings happen on the clock, on the same shift when we are normally scheduled to work.

When I worked at IAB, I was not eligible to be a grievance rep. In March of 2014 when I was promoted to lieutenant, I left IAB to work at the Patrol Bureau. I took the course to become a grievance rep. I felt my experience at IAB and my interest in mentoring people made it a logical role for me to take on. It is often a short-term relationship, maybe only one meeting, and I never know who is going to ask me to represent them next. A lot of people do this work, and it depends on what the officers need.

If an officer has been called to a meeting with their sergeant that might result in a disciplinary action, I can go with them as their rep for the meeting. My job is to make sure their contractual rights aren't being violated and that the interview falls within the scope of the investigation. We are entitled to see all documents and listen to the witness interviews the investigator has collected before our interview. I request everything and go over it with the focus, the person being investigated. If something hasn't been handled properly, I can object in our interview and help them file a grievance, which would then go through the proper channels.

One day, two white officers came to my office and told me they were witnesses in an investigation into an officer accused of driving under the influence of alcohol. They hadn't contacted a rep because witnesses don't usually need one. Before their interviews, the sergeant who would be interviewing them told them he also wanted to ask them why they had turned off their body-worn cameras (BWCs). Now they thought they were in trouble and needed a rep. They stopped by my office and asked for me to represent them.

I showed them the rules that state that they do not need to have their BWCs on when talking to another sworn officer; they had done nothing wrong. I went with them to the interview. The interview ended without the sergeant asking any questions about their BWCs. The officers were sure he didn't ask because I was there—he knew that BWCs were not in the scope of the investigation disclosed to them. So sometimes just having a rep in the room creates a better outcome.

Other problems aren't so easily fixed. I never know when I start a case whether it will be over in five minutes or if we'll still be fighting months later. It's not a problem for me when any officer needs help, because I am fighting an entire system of corruption and have to take the long view. I know that minority officers start out behind, and the system is not set up for us to win our cases.

Alicia is a Black officer who was temporarily assigned to the patrol office because she was injured and couldn't work in a patrol cruiser. She had experienced ongoing discrimination from her white supervisor, Sergeant John Burns. She got frustrated one day in October of 2016 when he asked her to process all the officer subpoenas for the day—a tedious, repetitive task that was usually shared by the team. She told Sergeant Burns that she was tired of being treated unfairly and that she would do half of the subpoenas. He told her he was tired of her complaints.

She left and went to see Commander Charles Lightfoot, the only other supervisor above the rank of sergeant working at that time. The rules allow division personnel to report EEO complaints to any supervisor. She told the commander that her sergeant had consistently treated her unfairly and this was the last straw. The commander sent her to another office to work for the rest of her shift, where she couldn't complete the assigned task. It was then his responsibility to write a letter detailing the issues and forward it up the chain of command. Commander Lightfoot did not write the letter as required.

She texted me because we had become friends while she was in one of my study groups. I had seen this type of frustration among minority officers before, but now, as a grievance rep, I was in an official position to help her. She was reaching out to me as someone who had been through the process before.

A few days later, while we were waiting for that process to play out, Sergeant Burns and his lieutenant opened up an investigation on Alicia for insubordination for not finishing the subpoenas. This was an act of pure retaliation and a serious accusation she could be fired for. Even though she had not been able to finish the task when the commander sent her to a different office, she still received a reprimand from the chief.

They never had any intention of investigating her claim of unfair treatment. I found her an attorney to represent her to file an EEO complaint with the Ohio Civil Rights Commission in November. Then both the OCRC and the division had to investigate it.

While Alicia was waiting for these two investigations to proceed, she was still working for Sergeant Burns. He was not reassigned, as sometimes happens when a supervisor is the focus of a discrimination investigation.

One day toward the end of November, Jennifer Knight, the Commander of IAB, the unit that is responsible for the internal investigation into EEO claims, drove over to Sergeant Burns's office. Knight stood within earshot of Alicia, two sergeants, and one sergeant in training while telling Sergeant Burns that he didn't need to worry about the EEO complaint because it had to go through her. She had heard the interview regarding the insubordination investigation of Alicia, which I attended as her grievance rep. She told Sergeant Burns that Alicia's EEO complaint was stupid and that it wasn't going anywhere. She also said she was going to take me out. This implied that she had already decided to find in his favor, even before her office had conducted their investigation. And she was already planning her retaliation.

Alicia called me very upset. I contacted the grievance chairperson at the union, who told me to have Alicia bring up the comments made by Knight at her upcoming interview with IAB. During the interview, the IAB investigator asked, "Has anyone retaliated against you?" She told him what Knight had said. The investigator was stunned—it is unheard of for a commander in charge of IAB to promise the outcome of an investigation in front of the person who filed the complaint.

I had taped this interview with everyone's knowledge. I met with the union grievance chair to let him hear the tape. He asked for a copy to take to a meeting with Chief Jacobs the following day, which he did. The chief then verified the story with the other two sergeants who heard Knight's promise to Sergeant Burns.

Chief Jacobs sent out a notice on January 17 that the commanders would be reassigned. Knight was out of IAB. Rhonda Grizzell was my new commander in Patrol. Jacobs, Knight, and Grizzell were known to be very good friends. I knew Jacobs had no choice but to move Knight after what she had done, but I didn't yet understand why I had a new commander.

What started out to be an opportunity to help a fellow Black female officer improve her working conditions was becoming much more involved. It seemed positive at first when Knight was removed from IAB. But I knew from my own previous EEO complaints that we might be in for a very long haul.

— 12 —

YOU'RE NOT GOING TO BELIEVE
WHAT THEY PULLED TODAY

Every time I took a stand, helped a colleague, or called out an injustice, they just found new methods of retaliation. It would be funny if it weren't so sad.

I had this funny feeling. Something didn't feel right. An officer warned me to be careful. I started saving e-mails and taking notes. Somehow I knew they were really coming for me this time. Then a couple weeks after the commanders were reassigned, on March 5, an officer told me Commander Rhonda Grizzell, my new white supervisor at the Patrol Bureau, was contacting Black officers and asking them to file complaints against me.

She's what!? That is not how it works.

I know all the rules, and I know I follow them. I wasn't worried about having an investigation stick. But still. I had never seen this kind of nonsense before—a commander talking to people several ranks below her, and not in her chain of command, to contrive allegations against me. This was a new flavor of retaliation that told me they were really mad this time. She was trying to get me fired.

On March 12, seventeen working days after Grizzell was assigned to be my commander, I was relieved of my assignment as a patrol lieutenant. In my two and a half years as the second-shift lieutenant for Zone 2, with two previous white commanders, I had never had any discipline issued, employee moral complaints, or EEO complaints. It took her two and a half weeks to make something up.

First she found one Black officer, Anthony Johnson, who would help her. You met him in Chapter Six—I had tried to help him with his habit of punching people. Then two others who had their own reasons to participate in this witch hunt jumped on board without much of anything to say. Then more. In an environment where it is hard to get ahead, I don't blame Black officers for feeling like they need to help out a commander. But she talked them into filing a complaint saying that I discriminated against Black people. Was she serious? The commanders knew there was only one type of complaint that would let them reassign me immediately while they conducted an investigation: discrimination.

The allegations against me allegedly occurred between two months and ten years before Grizzell even started the investigation. As officers, we are ordered to immediately report misconduct or be subject to discipline, however none of these officers was disciplined. The investigation consisted of an assortment of false allegations:

- Officer Johnson accused me of going to a drug dealer's house to tell the dealer to file a complaint on him, two years prior.
- Officer Jeff Kasza, a white officer, accused me of looking through his mug shots and stating, "You arrest white people too," ten years prior.
- Officer Paul Tobin, a white officer, accused me of stating to a citizen at a community meeting, "White officers kill Black people," several months prior.
- Officer Levon Morefield, a Black officer, accused me of calling him the N-word while talking to him on the phone, four months prior.
- Sergeant Andre Tate accused me of giving him a better performance evaluation because he is Black.

We call this the "CPD pile on." ("CPD" stands for the Columbus Police Department, our previous name and what Columbus folks still call us.) There were others, but these were the ones the investigator, Sergeant Dan Weaver, spent much of his time trying to prove. He concluded and wrote in his investigation that none of the allegations could be proven individually, but when taken together they were true. Now, does that make sense?

I was stripped of all my supervisory duties and reassigned to the property room. I had my badge and gun, so I was still a sworn officer, but I was working well below my rank in a job that was clearly retaliation for my work on Alicia's case. Normally sworn personnel who are relieved of assignment are placed in the patrol office answering phones. It is sometimes called "desk duty" in the media. I was the first person in the time I had been at the division reassigned to the property room and forced to do manual labor.

The new assignment was well beneath my training and capabilities. It involved removing the vest covers from the old bulletproof vests, taping the vest panels together, and then stacking them on pallets. The approximately one thousand vests were going to take months to complete. When I finished that, I would be cutting patches off of uniform shirts and cutting uniform pants in half. I reported to a civilian and had no access to a computer or my e-mail.

It was horrible, dirty, and demeaning. I hated it. They were clearly trying to punish me.

When I helped Alicia file her EEO complaint, I had warned her that her claim likely wouldn't go anywhere, because they never do by design, and then they would retaliate against her. It is a new experience for everyone with their first EEO complaint—they don't know what to expect or how they're going to handle it. I got a little more realistic with my second and third, but even I didn't understand how cruel they could be until I showed up for work the first day at the property room.

I packaged up my anger and frustration and channeled it into resolve and focus. It felt like I had gotten to the top of the mountain and figured out how to hold them accountable for their discrimination. I had even helped others along the way. And then, like an avalanche, I was back at the bottom—the property room.

I had plenty of time to plan my climb back up the hill. I was over halfway through law school at the time, which was such a gift from God. That experience and training gave me the skills and confidence to speak up. My attorneys, John Marshall and Sam Schlein, were with me every step.

In a strange twist, the union was on my side this time. The union represents all members, which they are required to do per labor law, but not always in the same way. Due to the seriousness of the case, the union provided me with an attorney, Jaci Tipton, and a grievance representative.

To start the process, on March 2, even before I was reassigned to the property room, Grizzell secretly recorded an interview she had disguised as a meeting with me. She had the HR/EEO manager, Miranda Vollmer, there but neglected to tell me I might need a union rep. I didn't learn that they had recorded the meeting until April 11. Per the union contract, I should have been given all the evidence they had against me before my Internal Affairs interview, but the tape was not presented. They played dirty from the very start.

As the investigation of the charges against me was beginning, Commander Knight was formally investigated for her interference in Alicia's EEO complaint. Even though Chief Jacobs had informally investigated this herself earlier, after the formal investigation she determined the accusation was unfounded, which means "the alleged conduct is refuted by a preponderance of the evidence." During the investigation Knight was never interviewed, even though she was the focus of the investigation. I had never seen that happen before. The witnesses were not interviewed. How can there be a preponderance of evidence refuting the alleged conduct if there was no evidence collected? This was Chief Jacobs's ability to manipulate investigations. Knight received no discipline. She was appointed to deputy chief by Chief Quinlan in 2020. Why would I expect anything else to happen?

Back in the property room, I reported to work each shift on time. Bulletproof Kevlar vests aren't that heavy, weighing from five to ten pounds each. But when they're stacked in piles, the weight adds up quickly. I was moving a pile of them one day in June of 2017 when a tremendous pain shot down my shoulder. I had blown out my rotator cuff and two discs in my neck. My doctor sent me home to recover. I took sick leave until our state workers' compensation benefits paid for my leave. The tear was severe enough to need surgery, but because of other health issues I requested nonsurgical treatment. I went to physical therapy and received shots for the inflammation while I healed. The recovery process was long and painful. I have some permanent problems and will never function at 100 percent again.

I wouldn't have asked for a shoulder injury, but it did get me out of the property room just when there was a lot of work to do to get my assignment back in Zone 2 patrol. In addition to law school classes and rehab, my days were spent preparing for grievance hearings, assisting with filing paperwork, meeting with my attorneys, and going to hearings. It was exhausting.

It seemed like every day they did something new wrong. I ended up filing seven grievances. Seven! That is ridiculous. I would have much preferred to just be doing my regular job. None of those cases were adjudicated properly per our procedures. They were all just rubber-stamped by the assistant public safety director, Doug Sarff.

By April of 2018, my shoulder was slowly getting better and the investigation against me was slowly proceeding. I was at home fully expecting to be returned to my position at some point. I signed up for the commander's exam to be given in June. It gave me a positive focus to survive the craziness they were putting me through. Passing that test would mean a pay raise, opportunities for more responsibility in different assignments, and the achievement of being the first Black woman in the history of the department to achieve that rank. That, combined with my law degree I would receive in August, would give me wonderful qualifications for several interesting and challenging assignments. I was ready.

I still had some limitations on my physical activities from my neck issues, including that I couldn't sit for longer than three hours at a time. I was going to ask for ADA accommodations to be able to take the test, or ask my doctor if it would be okay to sit longer, when the union called to say they had the chief's decision back for the EEO complaint against me. I met with them and they gave me the paperwork.

The chief recommended my termination on May 17, 2018.

Wait, what?! I hadn't done anything wrong, and now they were terminating me? My whole career, just gone? How did they think they could do this? I had been crying for a year waiting for justice to be served, and now this! I drove to the precinct and turned in my badge and gun to Commander Grizzell, who took great pride in accepting them. I can imagine she was thinking; *I got her. Not only did I get her out of her job, I got her out of the department.* She must have felt so proud of herself. I can imagine the joy that filled her heart to see that their plan to get me worked better than expected.

Little did she know, my mother didn't raise no punk.

By the next weekend, the department also told the world. There I was, on the evening news, in the newspaper, on the Internet, and on the radio as evidence that the Columbus Division of Police was doing something about racism.

> The Columbus Division of Police demoted
> Lieutenant Melissa McFadden in response
> to allegations that she created a hostile work
> environment and had a "black militancy mindset."
> Chief Kim Jacobs recommended McFadden be fired
> in May, following an Internal Affairs investigation.
> (WOSU)

This was the biggest psychological blow of the entire mess, and it seemed to be perfectly designed to not let me sit for the commander's exam. There was no way I could study now while I had to focus on fighting this devastating punch to the gut.

By June of 2018, I filed a federal discrimination lawsuit against the City of Columbus. That lawsuit is still in process as of this writing.

On June 27, I met with a group of pastors at Family Missionary Baptist Church who were also interested in hearing my story. I didn't feel like I was screaming into the wind anymore, and I was finding that people were interested in helping me find solutions to the racist environment I worked in. Twenty Black officers went with me to help the pastors see how widespread the problems were.

Since the division had gone public with this battle, I felt I needed to respond in kind. I went to the Columbus City Council meeting on July 16 and testified. Unbeknownst to me at the time, the IAB lieutenant and commander were in the balcony watching me testify. I told the council about the disparity in discipline, how complaints about discrimination are never sustained, how minority officers endure retaliation when we do complain, and that we needed help.

The day after I testified at city council, Chief Jacobs brought a new charge of untruthfulness against me. It was more nonsense accusing me of lying when I testified at the chief's hearing back in May that the officers who brought the charges of discrimination against me were lying. They went back to each officer and asked them if they were being truthful, which of course they said they were. So that supposedly made me untruthful for saying they were untruthful, two months prior, and coincidently the day after they watched me testify at city council.

It seemed that she was looking for a charge that would allow her to recommend me for termination again if the current dismissal was overturned. After several threats of more grievances from me and some urging from Safety Director Ned Pettus, Chief Jacobs withdrew the charges in September.

KIM JACOBS
Chief of Police

THE CITY OF
COLUMBUS
ANDREW J. GINTHER, MAYOR

DIVISION OF POLICE

September 4, 2018

Lieutenant Melissa McFadden #5039, L2B

RE: I.A.B. Database #201703-1015

Lieutenant McFadden:

This letter is to inform you that the disciplinary charges served upon you on July 26, 2018 for violations of Rule of Conduct 1.15(A)(5) and Central Work Rule 1 are hereby withdrawn.

Kim Jacobs
Chief of Police

KKJ/tcm

At a public forum on July 19, a woman came up to me to introduce herself. She said she had been a witness in the case against me. She was described in the investigation as the person I had been talking with when a white male officer supposedly overheard me say, "White officers kill Black people." In the investigation, Sergeant Weaver wrote he had not been able to make contact with her after calling her twice. The proper protocol to contact a witness is to send a certified letter after three phone attempts. There was no proof that they had followed this protocol.

When she came up to me at the forum, I told her I thought they hadn't talked to her. She said that wasn't true. They had called her and learned from her that I in fact had not said what was in the complaint. She was very sure of this because she said she would have argued with me if I had said such a thing. But the statement was still included in the investigation against me. My attorney contacted her and got an affidavit signed by her to attest to this.

Then I did a Facebook interview with a local activist on July 21. People I didn't even know started reaching out to me, offering to help. Also in July, Commander Knight began a rant on Facebook to complain that the union only represented me and not the officers I had been accused of discriminating against. Another officer commented that she should know better that the system doesn't work that way. She continued:

> **Marc Brill**
> Awesome reply Jeff. I to feel the same. So glad we just got the FOP back
>
> 2 hrs   Like   Reply   More

> **Jennifer Knight**
> I have been voicing my opinion and have always felt the Union provided the necessary balance to management rights. I have also done the right thing when the chips were down. I served on a contract team, voted, and tried to work with union goals not against them. What did I get Jeff? All this bought me nothing. Where has the union been when our officers were unknowingly recorded by a union rep and the tape was given to an outside party? Where has the union been as members has been attacked in the press by McFadden and called racist? The union has been silent for us but still works diligently to save her job. These are the issues that define an organization.
>
> 16 mins   Like   Reply   More

In July, I had a hearing with the safety director to review the chief's recommendation of termination. The union provided me with an attorney. We presented the affidavit from the witness. I had hired a national expert in Internal Affairs investigations to evaluate the validity of the investigation against me. His report detailed the many rules and procedures that had not been followed by the investigator. This expert concluded that:

> This investigation of allegations against Lt. McFadden fails to satisfy the ultimate mission of a reasonable and professional police administrative investigation of being unbiased, impartial, and objective.

It was obvious to everyone in the room that I had done nothing they accused me of. Even so, a few days later the union called saying they had received a call from the safety director's office asking what level of discipline I would accept. They said if I didn't pick a level of discipline that I could be terminated. Amazing!

I turned to my husband and shared what was happening. He told me that if I were terminated we would be fine, and he didn't want me to take the blame for something that I did not do. I told the union I would not accept any discipline because I had done nothing to warrant it.

The entire ordeal took eighteen months. The safety director restored my supervisory duties with no discipline and sent me back to my previous assignment as the Zone 2 second-shift lieutenant under Commander Grizzell. She wasted no time in giving me new reasons to file more grievances and a new EEO complaint. For instance, she told the sergeants working for me that they could bypass me in their chain of command and go directly to her. She would skip me and send investigations directly to my sergeants. She would not call me or answer my calls. All of our interactions were in writing or via voice mail. It was clear she was treating me differently than the other lieutenants under her.

On Martin Luther King Day in 2019, for example, I was invited to a prayer breakfast in the Black community sponsored by POER at First AME Zion Church. When we attend community functions in uniform, we need prior approval. I submitted the form and got approval.

I enjoyed my breakfast seeing old friends and meeting new people. As I was visiting, to my surprise, the president of POER invited me to come upstairs to join the pastors on the chancel. These pastors were aware of the work I was trying to do to improve policing in Columbus. I was humbled by their invitation and accepted.

The next surprise was that one of the pastors acknowledged my work and invited me to say a few words. I was embarrassed but stood up and said, "Thank you to the police safety director and the community." In those five seconds at the podium, folks in the audience took my picture and posted it on Facebook.

Grizzell went to the church's Facebook page to find pictures of me at the podium. Using them, she sent a letter up the chain of command to request another fraudulent investigation. She could have conducted the investigation herself but chose to use the process normally reserved for critical misconduct or complaints from the community. There had been no complaint received from anyone at the event. I was not notified that an investigation had been started—again. Several people who attended the prayer breakfast were interviewed about my participation in the event. Investigators even drove an hour to interview a police chief, a member of NOBLE, who had been at the event. After all that time and expense, the charges were determined to be unfounded and I received no discipline.

As with most complaints waged against Black officers, there are white officers being treated very differently. In the same month, a white sergeant, in uniform, gave a planned speech at a local bar association on overtime. He did not have prior approval for the overtime or for the speech. His case was not sent to IAB but instead investigated by his lieutenant who also reported to Grizzell. He was given the lowest level of discipline—a write-up (DCC).

As my new EEO complaint against Grizzell was in process, the EEO compliance officer had her removed as my supervisor. Those charges were unfounded, of course, but they did cause the rules to be changed to prevent supervisors from conducting targeted searches on social media pages without a specific complaint or permission from the chain of command. She went on to run the new unit in charge of officer wellness. I knew I felt better already!

When I was returned to my assignment after being gone for so long, the reaction of some officers I didn't know was surprising. One white officer came up to me and introduced himself saying, "It's a pleasure to meet you," like I was some kind of celebrity now. No one had fought back against the system before like I had and won.

At the first officer-involved shooting after I was back where I was running the scene, the detectives were overly complimentary at how I handled protecting the evidence before they got there.

I did what I had always done: learned the names and contact information for each person at the scene, secured the area, and then gave them a full report on the command bus when they arrived. It didn't feel any different to me—I just did the job I was trained to do. They were all looking at me strangely, so after I left the bus I asked the only Black detective there if I had done something wrong. He said no, that I had actually done much of their job for them. And the next day, even Chief Quinlan was complimenting my work to one of my friends.

This is what racism really feels like to me. We work with all the competence and professionalism we can gather, but no one sees it. They only see our Blackness and our defensiveness. When we prove ourselves as a worthy opponent, then they respect us. That was a lot of years, work, and legal fees just to get a few handshakes and high fives.

But I knew it couldn't last—the union had to remind me I was still Black. This e-mail arrived from their attorney:

From: Jaclyn Tipton <jtipton@hcands.com>
Sent: Tuesday, August 28, 2018, 3:56 PM
To: Melissa [McFadden]
Subject: Follow up

Melissa,

Just following up on our conversation. The Lodge has fully represented you through these charges (and continues to represent you in the untruthfulness charges to the extent that they are ongoing). Further, any civil suits are absolutely your right, and the Lodge is in no way trying to interfere in such suits.

However, if you make any public statements against specific members accusing them of racism or accusing the membership as a whole of being racist, the Lodge will have to defend the membership against such statements.

Thanks,
Jaci

— 13 —

CHANGING POLICY FROM WITHIN WASN'T WORKING

I had fought the system with small successes here and there, but the beast was bigger than I could battle on my own. I called in reinforcements, got political, and things started happening.

After the accusations made against me in the IAB investigation were not sustained, I was beyond tired of having this type of retaliation hurled against me. I finally decided I needed someone from outside the police department to help me affect change. At this point, the change would not be for me—it would be for everyone coming up through the ranks after me. Even so, I was determined to manifest significant change. I had not endured all the personal attacks for nothing. I watched the people who lied about me walk away with no consequences. I was really tired of it all.

The entire ordeal caused me to think about the structure of political power and who in the city both cared about the Black community and had clout at City Hall. As I focused on clergy members who cared about racial justice and had a following, my vision for change became clearer.

When Pastor Michael Reeves from the Corinthian Missionary Baptist Church and Minister Donell Muhammad from the Nation of Islam offered to go with me to city council and speak on my behalf about the racism inside the Columbus Division of Police, I no longer felt so alone in this struggle. Just meeting with them and having them not only listen to what we were going through but also offer to stand up to support us was overwhelming. I don't know what I expected would happen, but this response made me feel that I had a chance to bring others into this fight, and I would not have to go it alone. It gave me hope for the first time in a long time.

The Rev. Dr. Jefferey P. Kee from New Faith Baptist Church approached me after the meeting to tell me he has a degree in social justice and he was there to help me. We began holding community forums, but I realized that talking and having forums wasn't getting any change to occur. He encouraged me to call the Rev. Dr. Tim Ahrens of the First Congregational Church. They had worked together through a group of area congregations called Building Responsibility, Equity, and Dignity. Kee thought that Ahrens could call in pastors from other faiths to the effort. It was important to me that people from all races and faiths find a way to support the elimination of racism at the Columbus Division of Police. I knew that the pastors did not know me and they would need to see exactly what they would be fighting for. I started to put down my ideas in writing.

I began thinking through the processes that we would need to change to eliminate racism within the police. I wanted to make a positive impact on the officers that would in turn impact the community. I knew if I could explain the proposed changes well and back them up with evidence, the ministers would be ready to use their collective voices to lobby the mayor and city council for the changes.

If my many degrees have taught me anything, it is how to collect research (in policing, we call that evidence) and make a case for my position. So I started pulling records, talking to my fellow officers, and reading policies and statutes. I collected over five hundred pages of documents that explained the problems and defended the solutions I was proposing.

I settled on "Seven Expectations" as the title of my proposal that the clergy would deliver to the mayor. I picked seven action items that I thought would make the most impact with the least governmental action, contract changes, and minimal budget increases. I was trying to grab the low-hanging fruit but also make real change, knowing that there would be many more expectations after these goals were met.

On September 29, forty clergy members representing most of the faith traditions in the Columbus area met on the steps of City Hall for a planned press conference to sign and deliver the letter to Mayor Ginther. Several of them spoke to emphasize their personal and spiritual commitment to ending racism in policing. I did not attend because I did not want the spotlight—this was not about me. The ministers spoke on behalf of all the minority police officers and minority residents of Columbus. Having them gather to take up my fight made me feel the most hopeful and humble I have ever been in this struggle. The fact that they felt so strongly to speak publicly and sign their names made me believe that God had led me to do the things that I was doing and He led me to them. I knew I could keep going with His guidance.

The letter began:

> To: Mayor Andrew Ginther
> Date: September 29, 2018
>
> We, the undersigned religious leaders in the City of Columbus, submit the following recommendations for administrative changes to be made within the Columbus Division of Police (CPD) to benefit both the officers employed by the Division and the community they serve and protect. We expect to work with the Fraternal Order of Police and other interested parties to reach consensus for the benefit of all. It is obvious to all of us that not all officers nor all community members are treated with the same respect and dignity that we expect and that anti-discrimination laws dictate. We believe the following administrative changes will bring CPD into alignment with the will of the people of Columbus to treat all people fairly.

Even though this statement seems like a simple thing to say, the challenge of undoing racism is anything but simple.

As I've said many times, if we want police to start treating the public fairly, we have to start with our own behavior. So the first three expectations are an attempt to level the playing field for minority officers.

> **EXPECTATION #1** - Direct Equal Employment Opportunity (EEO) complaints to the EEO office within the City of Columbus Human Resources Department, instead of the CPD's Internal Affairs Bureau (IAB).

TV cop shows do a good job of painting IAB investigators as the good guys who root out the bad cops. Sorry, fake news, especially if the bad behavior was by a white officer toward a Black officer. Imagine your boss just did something totally inappropriate or wrong to you and the only person you can complain to also works for him. Imagine how far that complaint will get, and how much blowback you will get for making it. You now understand the need for Expectation 1.

Equal employment opportunity laws are not followed within the Columbus Division of Police. The microaggressions that minority officers experience every day rarely rise to the level where they can meet the threshold for an independent agency such as the Ohio Civil Rights Commission to find probable cause. The union, however, does not allow us to file grievances when we are discriminated against. The investigators at IAB who have no EEO training very rarely sustain an EEO complaint. Often the IAB investigator turns the investigation around on the person that complained about the discrimination, and they end up getting disciplined. We asked that the safety director establish a position for a trained professional who can process these complaints independent of IAB, like it used to be handled under Mayor Coleman's administration.

This was the first expectation that got public action. There was a national search for an assistant safety director with the title of EEO compliance officer. The job was filled by Kathleen Bourke. The request was for the discrimination complaints to be investigated independently of Internal Affairs, but Bourke's job is to sit in on the interviews with the IAB sergeant conducting the investigation. After all of the fanfare surrounding the search, she took her seat as an observer. The rest of the process is still the same. This still leaves minority officers with investigations that are slanted and the perpetrators of the discrimination with no accountability.

> **EXPECTATION #2** - Eliminate the subjectivity that currently affects the way Rules of Conduct violations are determined and discipline is subsequently dispensed. Predetermine the disciplinary action for each violation of the Rules of Conduct and apply the discipline uniformly. Implement the IAB Police Executive Research Forum (PERF) recommendations.

The Columbus Division of Police maintains a discipline tracking system. It lists each rule violation that occurs. It shows the discipline each officer receives for each violation. For example, the discipline tracking system shows for Rule 1.15, A.5: "Be truthful at all times," that this violation results in discipline of a termination or a major suspension. Any supervisor can pick the rule that they feel the person violated. And depending on the rule, they can determine the justification for harsher or lighter discipline. These three examples show how the outcomes can vary greatly:

- Joe Houseberg, a white officer, was untruthful about information on a special duty log that a private business relied upon to take legal action. Chief Jacobs changed the rule of conduct violation to 1.36, unbecoming conduct, and issued an 88-hour suspension.
- Jesse Perkins, a white officer, was untruthful about striking a suspect in the head with a baton. The FOP and the safety director reached a settlement of a 240-hour suspension.
- Michael Tucker, a Black officer, was untruthful about a person of interest taking a polygraph exam. Chief Jacobs terminated him.

The investigators can choose who they interview and in which order. This subjective process results in minority officers receiving much more severe discipline for charges of misconduct, and they have much less ability to defend themselves against these charges. Many community members of color who have been arrested will recognize this discriminatory behavior as well.

We asked that we eliminate the subjectivity of these disciplinary actions by requiring that we identify the conduct specifically. Then each person accused of a violation should be interviewed in the same order as every other investigation. We also need an external review of these discipline actions yearly to make sure they are finally handed out fairly. We have published complaints of this practice since the 1980s. It has never changed.

This expectation has not been implemented.

EXPECTATION #3 - Create an avenue separate from the CPD that Division personnel can use to report incidents of CPD corruption.

The Columbus Division of Police has been a corrupt and racist police department as long as I've been here and has likely been from the start. When I saw corruption, there was nothing I could do about it. Other officers tell me about the corruption they see. There was nothing I could do about that either—there was no one to report it to, really. The instructions were to report what we know to our immediate chain of command, who then reports to their supervisor, and so on. What are the chances that information will get where it needs to go to eliminate the corruption within the corrupt system itself? What are the chances the person involved won't find out who reported them? What are the chances that no one in that chain is involved?

It's so ironic, but we can't call 911 to report a crime. The best we can do is hope someone from outside the police department notices. Even if we go to the FBI or the attorney general, there is no whistleblower protection because we have officers working in task forces at all of those agencies.

We asked that a new process be established for reporting and investigating corruption that protects the whistleblower from retaliation. Isn't it amazing that this didn't already exist? Did everyone just assume that cops will follow the laws and police their own when they don't? I can't stress enough that this is a fatal flaw in policing that differentiates it from the military. You can't give military-grade weapons to people who have no accountability to themselves.

This request has been implemented. The language of Rule of Conduct 1.08 has been changed to read:

> Division personnel who become aware of another Division employee's involvement in misconduct of a criminal nature may also report the alleged misconduct to any law enforcement agency with proper jurisdiction, any regulatory body with proper oversight, or the Assistant Director – EEO Compliance for the Department of Public Safety.
>
> Any report of criminal activity by a Division employee, which is made either to a Division supervisor or to the Assistant Director – EEO Compliance for the Department of Public Safety, shall be treated as a report made pursuant to Ohio Revised Code 4113.52 (Ohio's Whistleblower Protection Act) and shall receive the protections outlined therein.

I haven't been able to use this new rule because everyone is well aware by now that I will be the first to write up or speak up about wrongdoing. They make sure to be on their best behavior when I'm around.

The next four of the seven expectations are for the protection of the public:

EXPECTATION #4 - Direct community (aka Citizen) complaint investigations conducted by the Internal Affairs Bureau involving racial profiling and discrimination to be reviewed by the City of Columbus EEO office for thoroughness, objectivity, and fairness.

Our mayors, police chiefs, and union presidents like to use the phrase "The Columbus Way," implying that we do it— meaning everything—better. The "it" in this expectation is investigating racial profiling and discrimination that has been reported by members of the community. The Columbus way to handle this is to take the complaint, go through the motions of an investigation, and determine ourselves to be not guilty. That keeps our record squeaky clean. Do that enough times and people stop reporting it, frustrated that it will lead nowhere and change nothing.

We asked for the EEO office at the city to review the work of the IAB to make sure we are not just creating a track record of little to no racial profiling and discrimination that we didn't earn. Then, when we say we are better than other cities, we can back it up with substantiated data.

Along with the creation of the EEO compliance officer in the safety director's office, there was an order that read:

> Upon completion of all investigations alleging discrimination against a member protected by the rights outlined in the City Charter, the Division shall forward a copy of the completed investigation to the Assistant Director - EEO Compliance.

We can only imagine what is happening to these copies, because no one has seen any reports yet. Maybe we forgot to say, "Read them, analyze them, and let us know how we're doing."

> EXPECTATION #5 - Require psychological counseling for an extended period of time, plus drug and alcohol testing, for officers whose intentional discharge of their firearm results in injury to others.

Most officers never shoot their gun in the line of duty. Some officers shoot their gun multiple times during their careers. When an officer uses their gun in the line of duty and shoots a citizen, sometimes they miss and sometimes it's fatal. The officer is required to meet one time with the division psychologist to determine if they are mentally OK to return to their regular duties. The officer has an incentive to say he or she is fine so they can return to work without any stigma.

Trauma specialists know that even one shot can rewire the brain to be more reactive in tense situations. This may go unnoticed until their reactions escalate to violent or fatal actions. We asked that officers who have shot a citizen be given mandatory counseling of their choosing to help them escape this cycle of violence before it starts.

If it was mandatory it would eliminate the stigma so that officers that need the help would actually receive it. In the past if the officer said something in the meeting that would cause the psychologist to determine that they were not handling the shooting well, the officer would have their badge and gun taken until their mental health issues were resolved. Even though that practice has changed over the last few years, there is still a stigma, and officers still feel compelled to make sure they say all the right things to get back to work.

They are not screened for drugs or alcohol after they use deadly force. The suspect that was shot or killed is tested for drugs and alcohol, so why not the officers?

As I write this, nothing has changed that would require ongoing counseling to any officer who has been involved in a shooting.

> **EXPECTATION #6** - Request that the State of Ohio Bureau of Criminal Investigation (BCI) investigate an officer's intentional discharge of their firearm that results in death.

When an officer shoots and kills a member of the community, the Columbus Division of Police has a responsibility to investigate that shooting and report its findings to the public. Over the years, as more unarmed citizens have been killed across the country, the public has grown weary of these investigations and has very little faith left in their impartiality.

We asked that police-involved shootings that result in fatalities to be assigned to the State of Ohio Bureau of Criminal Investigation (BCI) to carry out these investigations. The BCI is an agency that is available to local law enforcement to help with investigations they do not have the manpower or expertise to conduct themselves. The division conducts murder investigations routinely (due to our high murder rate in Columbus, unfortunately). But when our own officers kill, we are tasked with investigating ourselves. The community deserves to have fair, thorough, and transparent investigations done by an outside agency to rebuild their trust.

Once an investigation is completed, our county prosecutor, Ron O'Brien, presents the evidence to a grand jury. Between the evidence he is provided by the division and his instructions to the jurors, the grand juries have only returned one indictment against a police officer for murder or manslaughter in his twenty-four years in office.

This expectation was implemented in spring of 2020 as a response to the Black Lives Matter protests. It was expanded even beyond our request, to include all deaths occurring while in police custody. In his announcement, Mayor Ginther emphasized it was the first time this has ever been the procedure.

> **EXPECTATION #7** - Mandate that the Community Reconciliation Training course that will be submitted to and approved by the Ohio Counselor, Social Worker and Marriage and Family Therapist Board be implemented in each CPD Precinct.

My degree in social work taught me that when it comes to addressing systemic racism and community-wide trauma, the trainers at the division have no idea what they are talking about. They don't take specialized training; they merely learn from the officer that taught them. The world of social work research is constantly updating best practices and new insights into how policing can reduce trauma in the populations we serve.

As officers, we are supposed to help communities stay safe. How did we get to this moment when the most vulnerable people we serve feel traumatized by us constantly? When even the thought of being pulled over for a traffic stop can make someone panic, why aren't we panicking ourselves, looking for solutions from the most learned experts on this topic?

This expectation is asking for professionals from outside of the division to train both the officers and the community members that they serve in a combined training so that barriers can be torn down. It's a way for officers and citizens to truly get to know each other in an effort to build ambassadors on both sides.

This expectation has not been implemented. Various training initiatives have been proposed by the mayor's advisory council, the Police Executive Research Forum (PERF) report, and the Matrix report. None has required that the programs be combined to include citizens and officers.

When the pastors delivered the letter, they requested a face-to-face meeting with the mayor. Ginther met with them within a month and reported that he agreed with the Seven

Expectations. He had worked with his department heads to find out how each could be implemented, and he promised ongoing follow-up to work on these and other initiatives.

In the summer of 2018, Mayor Ginther formed the Columbus Community Safety Advisory Commission in response to outrage over the killing of young Black men by Columbus officers. During a meeting in June of 2019 when they heard testimony from the public, Sister Barbara Kane from the Dominican Sisters of Peace read the Seven Expectations to the commission members. Officers were given permission to attend too late to request the time off, so we wrote individual letters and sent them to Janet Jackson, the Black chair of the commission. She responded that she had read them but would not be distributing them to the commission members.

A couple months later, one of the commission members asked Jackson during a public meeting when the concerns of the minority officers would be discussed. Jackson responded that it had all been taken care of and the commission didn't need to do anything. When the pastors heard this, they scheduled another press conference and read each letter aloud in front of City Hall. I also sent the following letter to the commission members.

June 29, 2019
To Whom It May Concern:

I am writing this letter as a private citizen to help you understand the way female and minority officers are treated as employees of the Columbus Division of Police. I have endured 23 years watching the people in power manipulate a system that cultivates corruption, discrimination, and retaliation against officers who try to fight that corruption and discrimination.

Corruption occurs when the people in power are dishonest. When the head of an organization is dishonest, that dishonesty permeates the organization. That causes the safeguards in place to hold personnel accountable to erode. That, in turn, erodes the public trust. Minorities witness favoritism on almost a daily basis as assignments such as task forces, projects, and temporary assignments are offered to those who have gained favor with senior management. Recently, our chief sent a division-wide e-mail that stated:

> Some question why select individuals are frequently asked to take on more projects. It's typically because they have built a reputation of getting things done. And that's what I am challenging our sergeants and lieutenants to develop. A reputation of willingly accepting difficult asks and delivering a completed project on time and on budget while addressing contractual and regulatory processes.

This statement depends on all division personnel being given the same opportunities. As many of the letters and statements made by female and minority officers will attest to, opportunities to build a "reputation of getting things done" are only offered to a select few.

Further, when a job assignment is vacant, it is not required to be filled based on seniority. This results in a lower chance of a female or minority officer receiving that assignment. The highest-ranking personnel in the division condone this system that breeds unfairness.

Even when assignments are based on seniority, minorities (including females, Blacks, Latinos, and members of the LGBTQ community) often find themselves discouraged from taking assignments. They face intimidation, coercion, and retaliation just for applying for or accepting an assignment that they are entitled to have. Supervisors of the units often send intimidating e-mails or conduct unnecessary interviews in an attempt to discourage personnel from taking the assignment. Their goal is to assemble a group of like-minded personnel, in other words, personnel that they feel are "the right fit." Also, division personnel that are assigned to the unit will contact the applicant and discourage them from taking the assignment by sending the applicant text messages or calling them on the phone.

Back in the seventies and eighties minorities and females could only work certain units, which prompted the order from the judge in the POER v. City of Columbus lawsuit, to require parity in assignments for minorities.

Now, twenty-plus years later, threats and intimidation tactics keep minorities and females from taking assignments that they are rightfully entitled to.

- A female white officer took an assignment, based on seniority, after being told via multiple text messages that the unit wanted someone else. Posters were hung up at the substation in every stall in the female restroom, and the supervisor's office accusing the female of stealing the assignment from a male officer.
- A female Black officer applied for an assignment and was told that she would not get any training if she accepted the assignment.
- A male Black officer had a job application for another city given to him with his badge number on it, as a message that he was no longer wanted on that precinct.

- A lieutenant was directed to "talk" a male Black
  sergeant out of taking an assignment. The sergeant
  took the assignment anyway and filed EEO complaints
  due to the treatment that he received.

There are many other similar incidents that have
occurred over the last few years, but when minority
officers complain, no one is disciplined, therefore, the
behavior continues.

There should be a rule in place that prevents additional
interviews, phone calls, and e-mails to applicants for
assignments, unless it is specified in the job description
for that assignment. The Personnel Unit should be
tasked with contacting the applicants for the assignments
instead of the supervisors, in order to eliminate the
intimidation that often occurs when supervisors contact
the applicants directly.

Another issue that minority officers face is the huge
disparity in discipline. Females and Black officers
are disciplined at a much higher rate than their male
white counterparts. They also are often disciplined
much more harshly.

- A female Black officer and a male Black officer
  received a sustained allegation for failing to take a
  report out of an Internal Affairs investigation. Their
  sergeant and lieutenant recommended a documented
  constructive counseling (DCC), which is the first level
  of discipline. The commander concurred and also
  recommended a DCC, in which both officers were
  issued formal discipline.
- Two male white officers received a sustained
  allegation for failing to take a report out of an Internal
  Affairs investigation. Their sergeant and lieutenant

recommended a DCC. The commander disagreed
and gave both officers no formal discipline.

People may disagree on the punishment for this rule
violation, but most people will agree that they all deserved
the same punishment for the same conduct. Some
personnel receive termination for being untruthful,
where others receive a suspension. There is too much
subjectivity in the discipline process for an organization
that a federal judge determined to be biased against
females and people of color. The system needs to
be revamped to allow for discipline to be based on
conduct. Currently it is based on the investigators'
opinion as to which of the rules of conduct is the
better fit to apply to the person that they are looking
to discipline.

The current changes that are being made are
incremental changes that refine the status quo, not
eliminate it. The new leadership should be tasked
with making radical changes to fundamentally
shift the division's culture into one that respects
and values diversity within the ranks, which will
translate to respect and value for the communities
being served. A leader that is willing to make a
transformational shift to disrupt the culture of
corruption that is the Columbus Division of Police.

Sincerely,

Melissa McFadden
Private Citizen

So here we are, almost two years later, and we aren't batting .500 yet. The game is still rigged. It feels like we are back in 1985 but without a federal judge who has our backs. This list of reasonable requests, meant to help everyone, is still not all in play. The recommendations of the safety commission have not been implemented completely. The Matrix report was called out by ex-Chief Jacobs in August of 2020 as a waste of taxpayer money. Who could possibly disagree with all these positive, citizen-focused, anti-racist policy changes?

— 14 —

ACTIVISTS GOT ACTIVE

As the perfect storm of a worldwide pandemic and a series of normal racist atrocities made the news, a suspect in Minneapolis died on camera with the knee of a police officer pressing on his neck, and then Columbus police officers showed everyone how brutal we can be.

s long as I had worked at the Columbus Division of Police we had never had a phase 3 mobilization:

An emergency Division-wide mobilization authorized by the Chief of Police or a Deputy Chief that requires activation of the Emergency Operations Center, the designation of a Deputy Chief as the police incident commander, and may require cancellation of employee leaves and days off.

On Saturday, May 30, 2020, my commander called at 6 a.m. to tell me we were in a phase 3 mobilization due to the increasing unrest in the streets over George Floyd's death five days earlier. It was my first day off after working five—I was not that happy about it.

My first task was to call my sergeants, who would then call their officers to come in. We were putting together a "field force," a team consisting of one lieutenant and three to six sergeants, each with five or six officers.

With multiple field forces a commander oversees the lieutenants, who report to the operations section chief, who reports to the overall incident commander, who was Deputy Chief Michael Woods that day.

Operations like this also have special teams. An arrest team is two officers in a prisoner transport vehicle (paddy wagon). There are bicycle teams, SWAT teams, mounted teams on horseback, videographers, grenadiers (the specialists that launch the flash bombs and tear gas), and others as needed. It's a big operation. We had worked in field forces at many protests and at OSU–Michigan football games in the past, but this time the anger was directed at us, and we couldn't keep it together. By the end of the day, it was clear to everyone—including us—that we didn't know what we were doing.

I met my team at police headquarters where we picked up our riot gear and special weapons. I needed to submit the names of my three sergeants and their eighteen officers to the Emergency Operations Center staff to type into the roster. I had just finished that when Commander Kelly Weiner came running in yelling, "Get your riot gear and get out there right now! Broad and High! Broad and High! They need backup right now!"

The intersection of Broad Street and High Street is the crossroads of Columbus. It is one of the four corners around the Ohio Statehouse on the side where most protests are staged. Heading north on High Street takes you through the trendy arts/entertainment district called the Short North and then onto The Ohio State University campus. Heading west on Broad Street takes you to our beautiful riverfront and in the direction of City Hall and the police headquarters a couple of blocks away.

We put on our riot gear we call "turtle suits" and headed out. The first mistake was that we didn't have the color-coded stickers on our riot gear we use to tell each field force apart. When we are in those suits it is hard to tell who's who. We were off to a good start.

The officers with me all had long careers behind them. They were not there to wrestle or harass protestors. Honestly, they were just there to keep their jobs so they could retire soon. We had all been taught the effective ways that police can keep the peace during protests, and none of that was happening that morning.

The first thing that is supposed to happen in this situation is for the field force commander to contact the leadership of the protest and ask them what they are planning, what their goals are, and how we can help. We know that there are specific things that cause protests to turn into riots, and we are supposed to prevent those things as best we can.

The main issue is traffic flow. If protesters are walking, for instance, around the statehouse and we block their route, people will become angry. So it is the job of the police to make sure protesters are safe as they travel. We close the roads if we need to—the last thing we want are cars and pedestrians on the same roadway. Think about what officers do when a football game clears out and how we direct the pedestrians, close some streets, redirect the flow of traffic on others, and keep everyone heading home safely.

The challenge with protests is that they don't always know what they want before they start, or how many people will arrive and from which direction. But we know how to handle emergencies—we're the police. We respond to crises all the time that need immediate action. That's what we do.

Lieutenant Wade Spears and I, along with another lieutenant, each led a field force assigned the task of keeping protesters out of the intersection at Broad and High. We were preventing them from using the crosswalks as well. Eventually they got frustrated with this and moved west on Broad Street and south on High Street, creating a circular march across the streets and back. We would leave our posts at the intersection and chase them down to get them back on the sidewalks. This went on for quite a while.

Eventually the protesters got tired of being on the sidewalk, and a few of them started throwing water bottles. The field force commander ordered tear gas to be thrown. So, of course, that made the protesters disperse for a few minutes. When they regrouped, they started moving back and forth across the streets again. I suggested to the field force commander that we bring the bicycles in since those officers are mobile and my officers wouldn't need to chase the protesters around on foot. The field force commander didn't accept my suggestion.

After we chased the protesters around for a little while longer, another lieutenant told the field force commander that we couldn't keep chasing them around. He felt we needed to draw the line and if they crossed it, then we should take action. The field force commander took this advice, so the three field forces stood and held the line at the intersection of Broad and High.

After a few hours I went to the field force commander and asked if my field force could get relief. He told me that he would have to call Deputy Chief Woods and ask after he got off the phone with the mayor. A half hour after I asked for relief, Lieutenant Spears also asked if his field force could be relieved. The commander allowed it. Lieutenant Bill Laff and his field force came out to relieve Lieutenant Spears and his field force.

Once again, I went to the field force commander and asked for relief. I told him I had arrived the same time Spears had arrived. He said he would see what he could do. We had still not had any breaks for bathroom or food. Next thing I knew, Lieutenant Laff's team was sent back to headquarters, even though they had just gotten there an hour earlier. My field force had been there for five hours.

The intersection of Broad and Front is one block west of Broad and High and near Columbus City Hall. A large group of protesters had moved to that intersection. The other field forces left at Broad and High were reassigned to address the protesters who had moved. They formed another police line a block away at Broad and Front facing west. My job now included keeping protesters from moving west on Broad Street and surrounding the officers at Broad and Front from behind.

I looked around to find that two of my sergeants and their squads weren't there. It wasn't obvious until the other teams left. (No stickers, remember?) I called the Emergency Operations Center and learned that one had been reassigned to Spears and therefore left when he did. One had never been sent out but instead told to stay to guard police headquarters. Good to know. This left me with just one sergeant and six officers to hold the line at Broad and High. I told the EOC I needed to be relieved, since my field force commander was not responding to my repeated requests.

Then I looked up to see about five hundred protesters walking west on Broad Street, directly toward us. As they came toward us it was critical that we didn't let them pass us and box in the officers at Broad and Front. I screamed, "Hold the line! Hold the line!"

I had no idea what we would do if they wanted to keep moving down Broad Street. There were only eight of us and five hundred of them. We were understandably concerned. As they got to the intersection, a Black male with a bullhorn repeatedly told the protesters to stop at the police line. It wasn't obvious before then that they were going to stop.

Even though we train for these situations, it was clear to me that the protesters were much more organized than we were, with leaders who had a plan and a commitment to a nonviolent demonstration. As they stopped, I realized in my heart that they were only there to express their opinions and raise awareness for justice. Had they wanted to run us over, harm us, or cause any property damage, that would have been a perfect opportunity. There was nothing we could have done to stop them.

The EOC had finally gotten the message that my field force had been out too long. We were upset and needed to be relieved. They sent Lieutenant Laff and his field force right back out to relieve me.

I saw very little aggressive behavior from the protesters that day, maybe a couple of water bottles thrown in our direction but only after we stopped the flow of traffic and didn't let them use the crosswalks. The concern that I and others had was that we weren't prepared with the right tactics if we did encounter violence. First, we didn't have shields to protect ourselves as we protected the protestors. Second, we didn't have an arrest team that could remove specific protesters from the area to keep the event peaceful. And we didn't have flex cuffs if we needed to make mass arrests.

But my main concern was that I was effectively abandoned at a significant location to hold a line with too few officers. We know to never staff a field force with only one squad. I was the only woman and the only Black lieutenant in charge of a field force that day, reporting to a field force commander who was not responsive to my requests from the field. This particular commander has been known to not respect the women he worked with, and he had left us out there for over five hours without a break. Just from a tactical perspective, it was inexcusable. The lack of leadership was putting us and the protesters at risk. I will never know if this was just total incompetence or a deliberate attempt to put me in harm's way.

When I complained later that day that I didn't appreciate being left alone at Broad and High with one squad, a commander told me it was my fault because I had rushed out of the auditorium and left them behind. But Spears left at the same time I did, and they reassigned one of my squads to him. Police are usually good at just making up excuses for anything that goes wrong, but this one was nonsense. She was the one yelling at me to get out of there quickly.

The lack of leadership was apparent through the entire operation that day. For example, if we need to throw tear gas to disperse a crowd, the field force commander is supposed to advise us by uttering, "Gas, gas, gas!" and then half of us put on our gas masks while the other half holds the line, and then we switch. Seasoned protesters know to watch for this and often disperse before the gas is heading their way.

On this day, the field force commander abandoned our training. The only time I knew he was getting ready to disperse the tear gas was when I would see him wearing his mask. I never heard the warning over the radio. Since the protesters were loud, he should have used arm signals as well to make sure we were ready.

The same thing was supposed to happen when the horses came in. The field force commander should yell, "Horses, horses, horses!" The line then hinges like a door to let them pass. At one point, I was standing there and felt something brush my arm. I looked up to see a horse.

This operation was a total disaster for our leadership. We didn't do anything we had been taught to do to minimize the chance of a riot. Sadly, we didn't do everything we know how to do to keep personal injury and property damage to a minimum.

Instead we failed with basic leadership responsibilities that left officers free to operate with rogue tactics, like the inappropriate use of pepper spray on peaceful protestors. We are taught to use that weapon only from a distance of over six feet away and for a duration of only two to three seconds. The pepper spray is normally only carried by the sergeants, but that day for some unknown reason almost everyone was issued a large Mark 9 canister of pepper spray. The multiple incidents of brutal attacks on citizens for no justifiable reason are inexcusable. The next day, the mayor promised that no more chemical agents would be used, which was a good call to protect the protesters, but it was also because we were almost out.

At the debriefing after the shift, everyone was angry at our leadership. The response was terrible, and everyone knew it was terrible. I imagine different officers felt it was terrible for different reasons. I believe the day could have been a wonderful celebration of support for the Black community—I was shocked and delighted at the number of white allies that showed up. I had never seen that before. But my joy was dampened by the extreme show of brutality waged against peaceful protesters in Columbus that I had also never seen before. Even three of our Black officials, Congresswoman Joyce Beatty, Columbus City Council President Shannon Hardin, and Franklin County Commissioner Kevin Boyce, were pepper-sprayed that afternoon to the apparent delight of some of the officers.

In a police Facebook group, a number of Columbus officers were discussing the day's events. A friend sent me this screenshot. I am not a member of the group. They know

I would not tolerate this type of dialogue, especially on Facebook. In addition to three Black elected officials named in the last paragraph, they also reference our governor, Mike DeWine, and Mayor Ginther, who are white and in different political parties. The comments reflect the level of disrespect that peaceful protesters felt from Columbus police officers that day and for many more days of protest to come. The picture at the end they were proud to post is of Congresswoman Joyce Beatty in the heat of the altercation.

At this writing it is two months later, and the officers involved in this post are the focus of an Internal Affairs investigation, but no discipline has been issued. If it never became public and the division followed its historical behavior patterns, it would close out the investigation with minimal, if any, discipline. However, at least two of them have been disciplined in the past for inexcusable behavior.

I know some of my coworkers feel that the protesters deserved every injury they received and more. What they don't see is that it was our job to protect them, not injure them. We had all the tools and the power to make that day an amazing experience for everyone working to eradicate racism in the world. But instead we trotted out our best version of racist aggression and made sure everyone learned exactly how much it persists. The difference this time is that we showed white people how much it hurts—they have the bruises and the scars and the traumatic memories to prove it. We've been so good at hiding this brutality in the Black communities where there is less economic and political power to fight it. Bringing it out in the open just gave our new allies more resolve and gave the cause more political power.

For many in the Columbus Division of Police and the
FOP, the protest and the police response was just a fun
battle in the ongoing war against Black people. It was a
little inconvenient that white people showed up to help—
but that didn't stop the police from fighting a good fight.
When the mayor took away some of our weapons and told
us not to don our turtle suits the following day, they were
disappointed. The adrenaline was pumping, and they were
ready to keep fighting.

They can now take their fights to the outside law firm the mayor has hired to investigate the brutal acts committed by police that day. There is also a federal lawsuit already filed on behalf of several people injured by police actions during the protests. A citizen's advisory board has been seated to develop the process for a civilian review board to present to the voters for approval in November. This is in addition to the Ohio Bureau of Criminal Investigation that will now be investigating deaths of citizens caused by police officers. These are new battlefields that will hopefully expose even more of the racist culture that must be eliminated.

In law school I had the opportunity to study the Constitution more than ever before. I believe that the Columbus Division of Police violated the protesters' right to assembly. The Supreme Court has established that people have the right to say basically anything they want to the police and we should be able to take it. That is protected speech, and we are taught to deal with it. There is no higher purpose for police than to protect a citizen's constitutional rights.

On May 30, the police had a different purpose. The streets were not open that day, so what was the harm for everyone to be expressing their frustration over police brutality in the street? We had done our job to protect them from traffic hazards. There was no property to protect in the street. Who or what were we protecting by keeping them out of the street?

Our activists are finally protesting the entire division. There have been protests against specific actions of specific officers in the past, but this time the protesters are after the whole bureaucracy. At a minimum, they would like the institution of policing to stop the war on Black people. I would too.

— 15 —

WHO WOULD WANT
TO BE A COP?

Before I can look at a young Black girl or boy and honestly encourage them to be a cop, it will take everyone working together. We can't expect recruits to fix the racism within policing on their own.

Jackie, a Black detective and a friend of mine, along with two other Black officers were interviewed by the *Columbus Dispatch* for a video segment in July of 2020. The police department was rallying to defend their public image in the wake of the horrifying treatment of protesters in the George Floyd protests. Black officers are used for that a lot.

Jackie pointed out that a lot of the minority officers are at retirement age. She said now is the time for young people to come work in policing and make a difference. That is a true statement but a hard ask. There are so many youths in the Black community who would make wonderful community servants someday—they understand, from lived experience, many of the problems they would like to help solve.

These youths also know that police are causing many of the problems by harassing and locking up their friends and family members. They know that restorative justice would begin to rebuild the community and heal the wounds of centuries of racism. The division will need to make substantive changes to convince young people to join a profession they perceive as the enemy.

Jackie began her career in Columbus one year after the last group of officers was hired to fulfill the requirements of the Duncan decision. She is right that they will all be gone in a couple of years. Those of us who came after that hiring blitz trickled into the police academy without a clue that we were walking straight into a buzz saw that drew that thin black line between helping our community and keeping our jobs.

The division has a dismal record of retaining minority officers because only the strongest survive the racist attacks. We have each made a personal decision to confront the system of racism in the best way we know how, and we have supported each other as best we can. We've watched as so many officers were stripped of their guns and badges, and shook our heads as others willingly laid them down and walked out in despair.

I have watched the systemic racism in the Columbus Division of Police drive away dozens of good Black officers over the last twenty years. We just don't have enough Black officers and female officers yet to staff every unit equitably. If the division looked like the City of Columbus, we would have 400 more Black officers right now, 200 other officers of color, and 750 more women wearing a badge. We have a growing Latinx population in Columbus, but the Matrix report pointed out that their community feels that when their members pass the test to join the academy they are turned away for contrived reasons. Does that sound familiar?

Jackie and I and many other Black officers keep fighting the racist system that is still here thirty-five years after the Duncan decision. It is a system designed for Black officers to fail. Those of us who found ways to fight our way through it are proof that it can be done, but we are also proof that Columbus missed out on a great deal of productivity and creativity lost to lawsuits, grievance hearings, and even sickness that results from the everyday stress of navigating racism. We didn't get to move into assignments that challenged us in a good way. Instead we were demoralized by never achieving all the good we set out to achieve.

We could do very little except watch the police culture grow more and more deadly toward our own Black community. If we spoke out, we became the next target. Those of us who stayed to try to eliminate those risks are the target of anger from some in the Black community. That hurts the most, but I understand how it happened. I would feel the same way.

Do I want to invite Black youths to look forward to a career in policing? I would love to, but I want them to understand that they are not walking into a career that is ready for them to be equals. Black women especially need to work ten times harder to withstand the constant oppression. These young officers will need to seek mentors, organize, not rely on the union, stand up for themselves, and trust their gut when they see discrimination. Then they need to be ready for retaliation when they call out the racism. They will need to be aware that the white power structure will try to turn them against their neighborhoods. They will need to resist.

No one told me any of that when I was growing up—no one even hinted at it. I was ambushed. I'm lucky that I had my military experience to give me credibility and confidence. I don't think that the well-meaning people in city government and on citizen advisory panels truly understand the level of oppression and discrimination that still exists within the Columbus Division of Police. Part of that is because we haven't been able to tell the whole story until now. The other part is that they truly don't want to believe it. They are still in "bad apple" mode. It is really shameful that our police department is such a stain on our wonderful city that we love. I hope that learning my story will encourage them to make the substantial cultural changes that will let us all move forward with professionalism and pride.

In 2020, everything should not be about racism and sexism in the division, but it is. It spills over into our relationship with the people we serve. What is happening inside the division is a plague that has tragic implications in our community.

The more Black officers we have at a roll call, or at a crime scene or in chain of command meetings, the better. There are certain things that don't happen when we are there. It's a little like what happens when your grandmother walks in—you know how she and the Lord expect you to behave, but you just might not follow her guidance when she is not in the room.

I am pretty sure that the white officers who are thrilled to not be working with me see me as an unreasonable church lady who doesn't understand the real world. It is sad that there are those that need to be disciplined and reminded to treat everyone with respect. I certainly didn't ask for that job—I would have been happy if every sworn officer I've supervised had grown up on their own and arrived under my supervision ready to do the right thing. Some of their recent behaviors during the George Floyd protests are proof that some haven't yet found their own moral compass.

Every Black officer, especially the new recruits, might not feel empowered to speak out, but they do have a foundational knowledge of the existence of racism that changes the dynamic. With more mentoring, more allies, and more books like this, I hope more of them will feel empowered to speak up when they see white supremacy in a particular situation. As we saw with the George Floyd protests, there are more white allies showing up than ever before and they are listening when we speak like never before. But there is a lot that goes on that they will never know about unless we tell them.

The thing that has truly gotten me through it all is my faith in God. He set my moral compass to do the right thing, every single time. This meant that no one could ever prove any wrongdoing when they tried to come after me. In order to catch me, they had to lie about my actions. God prepared me to be ready when they came for me.

God sent me to the pastors when I needed to learn more about how to work through the evil I was experiencing. During the George Floyd protests, the pastors held a press conference that had 70,000 views on YouTube before the end of the day. They expressed their sincere disapproval of the behavior of Columbus officers, the racism that permeates the culture, and the lack of responsiveness to their earlier demands.

Sergeant James Fuqua, the public information officer, who is Black, responded to their press conference and said if any officers have any problems with discrimination that they can call him if they have concerns. He inferred that was the procedure and protocol for discrimination complaints, which is not true. This was his way of covering for Chief Quinlan's inadequate response to the systemic internal discrimination issues that the pastors and I had brought forth.

The pastors and many other activists will keep trying to hold the Columbus Division of Police accountable.

The politicians are hearing the pleas for reforms to policing. The most important reform is not to focus on the bad apples, but to support the good ones. There are many good officers who start this career thinking it is something very different.

Then they are swept up into the corrupt culture that begins its indoctrination in the academy and never stops. Even those who resist the culture have little power to speak out against it, as you have seen through my experience. Let everyone speak—until you know their stories, you won't understand what needs to be fixed or replaced. You might just be trading one bad apple for another.

From the first time my fellow officers heard me call them out for breaking a rule, they thought I was the bad apple. I didn't care back then, and I still don't. Their judgment of me is not important. It only reveals their abandonment of their sworn oath and their misreading of God's will. As I look back on my career, I am proud of the incremental changes that I was able to make. When my mom passed, she knew I was still fighting for justice the way she taught me. But I am disappointed in the fact that past injustices have not been corrected and atoned for. And the people responsible have not yet been held accountable. My hope is that this book will help bring about some type of true justice.

EPILOGUE

Just as I turned in this book to my editors, I filed my next grievance with the union. I just learned that the division has another database that is used to justify harsher discipline for Black and female officers. This story is not over.

Made in the USA
Monee, IL
13 April 2024

56900634R00125